New Products, New Risks

NEW PRODUCTS, NEW RISKS

How Bankers Are Adapting to the New International Marketplace

Paul M. Sacks

Samuel H. Crawford

Multinational Strategies, Inc.

HarperBusiness
A Division of HarperCollins*Publishers*

2-23-95

Library of Congress Cataloging-in-Publication Data

Sacks, Paul M., 1942–
    New products, new risks/Paul M. Sacks, Samual H. Crawford
      p.   cm.
    Includes bibliographical references and index.
    ISBN 0–88730–499–0
    1. Banks and banking, International.   2. Financial services
industry.   3. Risk assessment.   4. Banks and banking—United States.
5. Banks and banking—Great Britain.   6. Banks and banking—Canada.
7. Bankers—Attitudes.   I. Crawford, Samuel H.   II. Title.
    HG3881.C67445   1991   90–26985
      332.1—dc20   CIP

91 92 93 94 CC/HC 9 8 7 6 5 4 3 2 1

Contents

Preface

This book is about institutional change in the context of market change. It examines how a select group of commercial and investment banks has adapted to the significantly changed financial markets of the 1980s and their attendant array of new financial products and risks.

The subjects of our story are international banks, especially U.S., British, and Canadian institutions. Using nearly 100 formal confidential interviews and hundreds of informal conversations, we have traced the strategies that these banks have adopted to stay afloat, remain competitive, and sometimes thrive in the new environment that emerged in the early to mid-1980s.

The period in question is a watershed in the development of postwar financial markets and the banking industry itself. Its start was marked by the debt crisis of 1982, a peroration that has conditioned most if not all of what has followed. Beyond the immediate effect of the debt crisis, great changes have shaken both the markets and the industry: deregulation followed by reregulation; the emergence of internationally coordinated efforts to create a level playing field and govern the behavior of the players; the emergence and refinement of international telecommunications capabilities, which undergirded the movement toward global products and global management; and the widespread use of computer systems in creating, vending, and managing increasingly mathematical and structured products.

Admittedly, many of the most important risks of the business remain unchanged. Banking remains rooted in the traditional function of lending to borrowers who, in the banker's best estimate, are likely to make good on their obligations. Many of the most serious financial crises occupying the news at the time of writing involve the dubious quality of those estimates: the U.S. thrift industry debacle is but one example. Banks still can and do, as one banker put it, "lose money in the stupidest and most conventional ways."

Yet innovation in the 1980s has transformed the industry. Once a comfortable business conducted in a conventional way and, assuming prudent practice, characterized by fairly predictable and healthy returns, banking has become a highly competitive enterprise requiring risks that often are greater than before, usually are less well known than before, and are taken on in pursuit of ever narrower margins.

In the process, many gentlemen and a few ladies have passed by the wayside, yielding their places to "quants," "financial engineers," and the like. Revered private institutions have gone public in search of capital, often revealing severe management shortcomings. Traditional industry leaders have seen their positions eroded while new institutions have come to the fore. Markets have collapsed and new markets have been built; some, like the junk-bond market, have flourished only to be tested, in turn, to the point of collapse. The very center of banking gravity has fragmented, yielding to a decentralized structure that tests the competitiveness-enhancing or competitiveness-inhibiting characteristics of national systems and the ingenuity and political talents of national regulators.

Whatever else can be said for this period, it has not been boring.

This book rests substantially on extensive formal and informal conversations with senior bankers over the past several years. Their respective institutions all bear names known throughout the world; all are large banks heavily involved in international business; in their respective countries all occupy what is generally considered to be the promontory of high finance. These executives frequently regarded their institutions as highly visible entities operating within markets and industries subject to close administrative review and regulatory control. Their resulting reluctance to speak on the record is understandable but may frustrate the careful reader. We apologize for our many opaque references, and can only point out that without such circumspection on our side, no book of this type could have been written.

The focus of this study is narrower than we might have wished. First, we regret the absence of Japanese banks from the study. As most observers of the scene recognize, Japanese banks characteristically are more reticent than their U.S. or European counterparts about disclosing confidential information. We respect this posture, but because we could not talk as confidentially with Japanese banks as with other institutions, we could not properly report on them. We therefore made the decision to omit them from the book.

Second, we have excluded Continental banks—notably, the major German, Swiss, and French institutions. In so doing, we have created a study that may justifiably be charged with the Anglo-Saxon parochialism that often colors the industry itself. Our failure to incorporate these banks into the book stems from the circumstances surrounding our research, much of which was undertaken prior to mid-1988—the moment when business, and U.S. banks in particular, awoke to the promise of European markets and the potential competitive presence of European institutions. Prior to mid-1988 the Continent held little allure for our clients, whose interests dictated the direction of our research; after mid-1988 publication deadlines for this book would have been breached beyond repair by a *de novo* approach to prominent Continental institutions.

Readers of contemporary banking literature will recognize many of the published works and authorities cited here. Referencing supplementary material reduces the overall opacity of the text and, we hope, allows a straightforward presentation of organizational stress and accomplishment during a transitional period.

The book also reflects several years of related research commissioned by Multinational Strategies' clients. Table P. 1 provides an overview of the extent and focus of the landmark projects of that research.

TABLE P.1

Multinational Strategies Research

Study	Year	Type of Institution	External Market Events	Internal Business Trends
"Country Risk"	1983	U.S. money-center commercial banks	1982 debt crisis	Creation of internal debt bureaucracy
"New Products, New Risks"	1985	U.S., U.K., and Canadian money-center commercial banks	Market deregulation throughout the OECD	Shift to merchant banking
"Investment Banking: Competitor Analysis"	1986	Top-tier U.S. and European investment banks	Big bang; globalization	Capital raising; international expansion
"Regional Banks"	1987	U.S. regional banks	Deterioration in bank credit quality and emergence of regionals as a force in the United States	Redefinition of business strategies; retreat from international business
"New Products, New Risks: A Reprise"	1988	U.S., U.K., and Canadian money-center banks and U.S. investment banks	Credit boom, late phase; international reregulation	Retrenchment and consolidation of global ambitions

Acknowledgments

We want to thank our many valued collaborators in this effort.

Chris Canavan's analytic skills greatly enhanced the material presented in chapter 3; we grudgingly acquiesced when, during the early stages of this project he began a long-planned leave of absence from our shop for a stint at Columbia University. We would also like to thank Michelle Miller and Vicky Stein for their help on an earlier version of this essay.

Most important, however, are the many bankers whose conversations are reflected here and the institutions for which they work. In a very real sense, this book is the result of relationships built over nearly two decades between Multinational Strategies and the banks these managers represent. The events of the 1980s intensified many of these ties, as MNS found itself increasingly called on to expand its earlier role as an advisor on international business climates and transactions to include advisor on management of Third World debt.

The mutual trust that has evolved through these interactions provided the bedrock for our research efforts on this book, and we were repeatedly impressed by the generosity of respondents who gave us their time and insights. Their industry is a difficult one to understand and to portray. We hope that some, at least, will feel that we have done a serviceable job of representing their dilemmas, failures, and successes.

List of Abbreviations

ATRR	allocated transfer-risk reserve
BBA	British Bankers' Association
BIS	Bank for International Settlements
CMO	collateralized mortgage obligation
COMEX	Commodity Exchange
EEC	European Economic Community
FHLMC	Federal Home Loan Mortgage Corporation (Freddie Mac)
FNMA	Federal National Mortgage Association (Fannie Mae)
FRN	floating-rate note
GNMA	Government National Mortgage Association (Ginnie Mae)
ICON	indexed currency option note
IMF	International Monetary Fund
IO	interest-only bond
IPO	initial public offering
ISDA	International Swap Dealers' Association
LBO	leveraged buyout
LDC	less developed country
LIBID	London interbank bid rate
LIBOR	London interbank offered rate
LIMEAN	London interbank mean bid and offer rate
LME	London Metals Exchange
LTCB	Long Term Credit Bank of Japan
MIS	management information system
MNC	multinational company
MOF	multi-option facility

NIF	note issuance facility
OCC	Office of the Comptroller of the Currency
OECD	Organization for Economic Cooperation and Development
OPEC	Organization of Petroleum Exporting Countries
OTC	over the counter
PO	principal-only bond
REMIC	real estate mortgage investment conduit
RUF	revolving underwriting faclity
S&L	savings and loan association
SEC	Securities and Exchange Commission
SNIF	short-term note issuance facility
STIF	short-term issuance facility
T-bond	treasury bond
TRUF	transferable underwriting facility

1

The New Environment

The business of banking has changed and with it the nature of bank risk. At the level of the institution, our abiding concern in this essay, the changes have come swiftly. They have often been defensive in nature, as both commercial and investment banks have struggled defensively to adapt to changed circumstances and replace diminishing sources of revenue, and they have often been predicated on an understanding, itself uncertain and influenced by misperceptions, of changes in the international marketplace. As such, the changes have not been always consistent or unidirectional. The picture that emerges is not one of steady progress. A good deal of the story we are about to tell concerns strategic rethinking, discarded tactics, and the recognition of error.

Changes in the way commercial and investment bankers go about their increasingly similar businesses occur within and are related to a highly complex and interwoven network of change occurring in institutions, markets, national systems, and the international financial order. Buffeted by the debt crisis, disintermediation, increased competition stemming from domestic deregulation, higher cost of funds, and lower spreads, commercial banks have sought to execute a tricky pincer maneuver—between the imperative to cleanse their balance sheets and the need to develop new sources of revenue with minimal commitment of term credit.

Banks have retreated from much of the international expansion they undertook in the 1970s, notably voluntary sovereign lending, while at the same time being drawn into an intimate involvement in the economies of less developed countries (LDCs). International operations have been restructured, and retrenchment is visible in virtually every institution. Active asset management on a large scale—loan trades, swaps, and outright sales—has replaced the stable business of managing credit relationships. Today banks are frenetically competing to offer new, fee-earning financial products and, as a result, have come under increased scrutiny from shareholders and regulators. The Glass-Steagall Act and McFadden Act, twin pillars of U.S. banking, have been eroded by clever and diligent lawyering primarily sponsored by New York–based money-center banks: outside the United States under the spur of market stimuli the same intermingling of traditionally separate areas of commercial and investment banking has occurred with greater speed and lower legal overheads.

Beginning in the 1970s but accelerating recently, investment banks as well have seen their traditional markets, protected by legal and regulatory separations, become porous and open. As the market once characterized by highly imperfect competition has significantly lowered barriers to entry, these institutions have been forced to change. Trading has greatly increased, and new capital has been sought—to support not only larger trading and underwriting positions but also new merchant banking activities requiring large commitments of capital in buyouts and loans. Capital also supports heavy multi-year investment programs designed to expand staff and equipment in major and minor financial centers. Of the leading investment banking institutions in the United States, Canada, and the United Kingdom entering the 1980s as private partnerships, nearly every one became either a publicly traded corporation or part of a larger corporate entity by the end of the decade. The same phenomenon is visible throughout the Organization for Economic Cooperation and Development (OECD). The changes are virtually universal.

Finally, supervisory authorities have had to reorient themselves. Old regulatory approaches rooted in legal separations of the activities permitted to types of institutions are in the process of being reworked to account for the substantial similarity of activities being pursued by commercial banks, investment banks, nonbanking financial companies, and even nonfinancial conglomerates with financial subsidiaries. As supervisory authorities are entrusted with maintaining sound and stable systems in an international system, cooperation between national authorities is complicated by the political pressures on trade issues as applied to trade in financial services.

The Revolution in International Banking

The revolution in international banking is fueled by the lower profits available in traditional banking markets. As those markets have become considerably less lucrative, novel and unconventional financing techniques—such as interest-rate swaps, loan swaps, note facilities, revolving underwriting facilities (RUFs), multi-option facilities (MOFs), Eurocommercial paper, and other new products—represent increasing percentages of new financings on a global basis.

Financial innovation has its costs, however: top international bankers agree that banks have assumed new and not yet fully understood risks. Many new products have not been tested by a full business and interest-rate cycle; many are based on lawyers' best efforts but have not been scrutinized in court; others, such as portfolio insurance, have met with a bad end. Markets have disappeared and liquidity dried up at critical moments.

A change in the predominant attitude toward risk has been an important part of the overall revolution. Risk has ceased to be apprehended only or primarily as a potential danger to be avoided or cushioned and has become instead an economic commodity (often expressed or measured as price volatility over time) to be packaged and sold to a clientele only partially and occasionally aware of its consequences.

The changing nature of risk and changing institutional appetites for risk have had far-reaching effects on the ability of analysts to understand and guide financial institutions through the kaleidoscopic world of international capital markets. A risk-analysis gap has opened between the changing nature of international banking and traditional approaches to and techniques for gauging risk. Bank regulators around the world are increasingly concerned with these new risks and focused on their implications for banks' capital adequacy. Although most institutions have identified their own risk-analysis gaps, few banks have closed the gap to their own satisfaction. This lag between the changing nature of risk and bankers' ability to understand risk may be structural, given the rapid pace of innovation and change in the market, but the gap must close if banks are to continue enjoying the confidence critical to their survival.

The Changing International Regime

Bank internal control functions (such as audit, credit, and country-risk analysis) have been slow to adjust to an international banking that today is conducted in a wholly different environment than it was a decade ago. One measure of these changes is the set of rules governing international economic relationships—what has come to be called the international economic regime. Changes in this regime—some of which are outlined below—have affected international banking and altered the demands placed on the banks' internal "watchdogs."

A Pronounced Cycle of Inflation and Disinflation

Events in the U.S. economy mirror a more widespread phenomenon. In the 1950s inflation was stable at around 2.5 percent and remained so through the end of the 1960s. In the 1970s the rate of inflation accelerated to reach double-digit levels in 1979. The inflation rate increased again in 1981 before coming down sharply to about 2 percent before increasing again to the current level of around 5 percent. Martin Feldstein, former chairman to the Council of Economic Advisors, is not alone in viewing this cycle as the chief cause of many current banking problems. It made the deregulation of interest rates inevitable, skewed the credit-allocation and asset-pricing decisions of banking institutions in a number of ways, and greatly contributed to the process of the disintermediation of banks by depositors.[1]

Globalized Economic and Financial Markets

Although currently out of favor, the term *globalization* still describes today's tightly linked markets. Money has become more fungible with widespread electronic transfer, and money velocity appears to have increased. Percentage increases in the sum of traded money have greatly outstripped comparable increases in the sum of traded goods for the past five years, denoting the gradual detachment of banking from the groundwork of the real economy. At least two substantial market declines, in 1987 and 1989, have left no room for doubt about the linkage of markets: ease of entry and exit has lent itself to overtrading, and as MIT economist Charles Kindleberger once noted, "Overtrading has historically tended to spread from one country to another. The conduits are many."[2]

A Persistent National Context

While international economic interdependence has heightened enormously, the system is still dominated by national players and perspectives. Sophisticated analysts of bureaucratic change, such as Morton Halperin and Graham Allison, have long noted the fundamental tendency of bureaucracies to reproduce the status quo, which in this case is influenced by the interests of national governments. In reconciling the need to protect national interests in a market situation characterized by newly permeable national frontiers, bank supervisors have responded with remarkable coherence.

The challenge of adaptation continues. At present, the strong infusion of trade competitiveness issues into forums and discussions conventionally structured around the stability of national

[1]Martin Feldstein, "Strengthening the American Financial System," in Giacomo Luciani, *La Finanza Americana Fra Euforia e Crisi* (Milan: Fondazione Olivetti, 1989), pp. 1–12.
[2]Charles Kindleberger, *Manias, Panics and Crashes* (New York: Basic Books, 1978), p. 18.

systems creates contradictory and sometimes volatile pressures. Supervisory authorities, particularly central banks, have always needed to be politically canny, just as they have had to carefully maintain a credible political neutrality. Sustaining this difficult balance will not become easier in the foreseeable future.

An Expanded Institutional Role for International Banks and Multilateral Development Banks

The roles of private international banks and multilateral financial institutions have been enhanced, a situation that more than one observer has characterized as overreaching. One consequence of the sovereign lending spree of the 1970s and the debt crisis that ensued was that banks hold a structural stake in and influence over the domestic economic adjustment policies of major debtor nations. In some respects this new power relationship resembles the receivership situation that banks find themselves in when they are thrust into management responsibilities for troubled companies.

In effect, an era of receivership has been inaugurated. Debtor nations are forced to submit the apparatus of domestic economic policy making to the dictates of the International Monetary Fund (IMF), the Bank for International Settlements (BIS), and the large number of private syndicates that have loaned money to them. This can only result in economic hardship for the debtors as a large and unwieldy group of lenders assumes responsibilities beyond the scope of its competence and experience.

To some extent, this situation appears self-liquidating: the debt links between private banks and countries are weakening as syndicated sovereign lending declines. This has certainly characterized U.S.–Latin American banking relationships during the Baker plan period. The opening of Eastern Europe, however, indicates that it is premature to assume that sovereign debt problems have been put to rest. The debt crisis may simply be entering a new phase, one where most banking protagonists are Continental and not American.

A Changed U.S. Role in the World Economy

The economic influence of the United States continues to be strong, but it has changed. Today the U.S. role is increasingly one of a market rather than a donor. The role played by the United States as a provider of new investment and foreign aid has declined, while its role as a major market for foreign capital and exports and as a safe haven for foreign direct investment has vastly increased. The number of institutions having a stake in preserving this situation has grown substantially as well. The health and permeability of the U.S. economy thus assume new relevance to international banking activities.

The Changing International Capital Market

These basic changes in the international regime have occurred concomitantly with profound changes in the structure of international capital markets.

Pressures on Market Structure

Structural changes reflect two basic developments. The first is a set of new market circumstances—troubled debtors, declining interest rates, market deregulation, increasing competition among institutions, disintermediation, and the spate of new mergers and acquisitions. The second development is a reaction to the first—the new emphases and strategies of the key players. Institutions operating in international capital markets have been swift to adapt to these challenges by developing new financial products to meet current financing needs. This unparalleled pace of financial innovation has prompted concern among bank managers that the new risks being assumed are inadequately understood.

Structural Trends

Several primary trends in international capital markets can be noted.

Deregulated International Capital Markets.　The deregulation of financial institutions, for several years a trend in the United States, is now being paralleled in other markets. As the Japanese move toward market liberalization, deregulation and liberalization have taken hold in countries such as Australia, the United Kingdom, France, and Italy. This opening of markets has resulted in heightened competition and reduced intermediation costs, and has contributed to the mushrooming of new financing techniques.

Declining Traditional Forms of Financing, Especially Syndicated Lending.
In 1986 the analysts of the OECD announced the trend, writing,

> Over the past four years, the combined share of the "traditional" borrowing vehicles—straight bonds, internationally syndicated credits, and offerings of convertibles—has shrunk from over 85 per cent to around 58 per cent. The decline has been extremely pronounced in the case of the international syndicated loans proper which last year accounted for only some 22 per cent of total financing as compared with 57 per cent in 1981–82.[3]

A significant component of this decline has been the virtual demise of voluntary sovereign lending to developing countries. Instead, the bulk of new lending has helped to restructure and refinance old syndicated debt. Flows of funds from the troubled debtor countries have been negative since 1982. Thus low demand for syndicated loans (as the poorer debtors are unable to access the market and the better-quality ones seek cheaper forms of financing) has furthered a dramatic change in international lending activity, and the change has influenced institutional strategy, management policy staffing levels, and risk control.

Disintermediation.　Disintermediation, or the removal of banks as intermediaries in the accessing of capital markets, usually by the issuance of commercial paper, reflects two operating realities: the relative efficiency of capital markets compared with banks in

[3]Organization for Economic Cooperation and Development, *Financial Market Trends* (November 1986): 50.

providing funds to quality borrowers, and bank credit quality has eroded, implying that commercial bankers' best corporate customers enjoy a better credit rating than the bank itself. Disintermediation has occurred at varying rates throughout the OECD. It has been complete in the United States, Canada, and Britain for some years now and continues to advance in Italy and France. It is relatively new in Germany because of the close relationships between German banks and German companies and in Spain because that country still has a relatively underdeveloped capital market. It has constituted an important push factor in the pace of financial competition.

Increased Competition. Overcapacity and increased competition have ushered in what economist Joseph Schumpeter describes as a phase of "creative destruction."[4] The failures of individual firms occur within a broader context of market change and renewal. As the increased permeability of markets and lower barriers to entry cause some firms to go out of business, the most dangerous associated phenomenon is the possibility that firms will lower business standards in order to survive—specifically, that financial firms will weaken their internal prudential rules to maintain competitiveness. To some extent, this has occurred, and the reverse process of rebuilding prudential standards is underway, although overcapacity still characterizes most financial markets.

Innovative Financing Techniques. Table 1.1 shows some clear trends. Gross borrowing overall increased sharply in the 1980s, and the shares of borrowing related to the syndicated loan market have fallen off dramatically. The brief reprise in 1987 and 1988 coincides, not accidentally, with a tremendous upswing in merger and acquisition activity (over 60 percent of such borrowing in 1988), principally in the U.S. and U.K. markets. This temporary blip

---

[4]We are indebted to Rainer S. Masera, who elaborated on this idea in a paper, "Issues in Financial Regulation: Efficiency, Stability, Information," presented at the Société Universitaire Européene de Recherches Financières Colloquium on *Financial Institutions in Europe* held in Nice, October 12–14, 1989.

does not confute the trend of shrinkage. Even more to the point are the increased percentages and absolute volumes of borrowings achieved through instruments in the third group—a rough approximation of the new instruments.

One consequence of this frenzy of financial innovation has been the acceptance of new and unknown forms of risk—directly, by venturing into higher-risk credit activity, and indirectly, by weakening each institution's internal control system. The first line of defense in ensuring the safety and stability of financial institutions rests with their own mechanisms of internal control.

New Geographic Focus. In addition to the creation of new financial products, there has been a substantial shift in geographic emphasis on the part of international banks (see table 1.2). New voluntary lending to troubled debtor countries has all but dried up; in its place has come more lending (and financing activity) for Asian countries and "quality" (i.e., OECD) borrowers). This, in turn, has affected the work requirements of risk analysts.

TABLE 1.1

Borrowing on International Capital Markets by Major Instruments

Instruments[a]	1984	1985	1986	1987	1988
Syndicated loans	23.2 %	12.8 %	13.6 %	20.9 %	26.7 %
Straight bonds	29.6	33.7	36.3	30.9	35.8
Equity shares	—	1.0	3.0	4.6	1.7
Other bonds	2.0	1.6	2.2	1.0	0.5
Eurocommercial paper	—	4.5	15.2	14.2	12.6
Floating-rate notes	19.4	20.9	13.1	3.3	4.9
Bond/equity hybrids	5.5	4.0	6.9	6.3	6.3
Note-issuance facilities	8.8	12.2	6.4	7.4	3.2
Other back-up facilities	5.8	3.0	1.1	0.5	0.5
Total[b]	$183.2	$263.2	$380.9	$350.1	$416.2

SOURCE: Organization for Economic Cooperation and Development, *Financial Market Trends* (November 1987, May 1989).
a. Consistent and continuous data are not available on all the new instruments because many were off balance sheet prior to 1987, and subsequent data collection is still sketchy. The percentages do not add to 100 owing to intentional authors' omissions.
b. All amounts are in billions of U.S. dollars.

Looking at the syndicated loan market, the main shifts in geographic focus are

- *A flight to quality.* Since 1981 the share of funds going to OECD borrowers has risen from one-half the market to four-fifths;

- *Less financing for developing countries.* The aggregate amount of funds raised by developing countries has declined every year to 1987, when Baker plan–managed lending blipped up, only to fall off again in 1988 and 1989. This involves the virtual disappearance of Latin borrowers, a decline in the volume of borrowing by African and Middle Eastern countries, and the bulk of the remainder flowing toward Asian borrowers (primarily South Korea and Indonesia);

- *More financing for Eastern European countries.* Eastern Europe is the only underdeveloped region recording an increase in the period (1984), and its market share in future years can be expected to increase.

In addition to shifting the geographic mix of syndicated lending, banks also shifted the mix of existing loan portfolios by selling assets and swapping loans. The volume of this activity was rumored to have reached over $80 billion by 1984; the pace of increase has been substantially maintained since that time.

New Products for New Markets

International banks have dominated the reshaping of international capital markets. As new financial products have evolved to accommodate shifting rules and market conditions, they have affected the job of the risk analyst and the ability of banks to control risk.

These new products also have spurred a series of increasingly comprehensive regulatory actions. In April 1985 the Federal Reserve Board warned about the risks implied in off–balance-sheet banking and cautioned that as a result "primary capital ratios have looked cosmetically high." It further warned that "if banks

TABLE 1.2

Medium-Term External Bank Loans

Borrowers	1982[a]	1983	1984	1985	1986	1987	1988
OECD area	$54.8	$54.8	$32.0	$32.5	$36.3	$66.8	$103.8
Eastern Europe	0.6	0.6	1.0	3.0	2.7	2.9	2.7
OPEC	8.0	8.0	7.3	3.3	3.5	2.2	1.3
Other LDCs	32.5	32.5	24.9	19.6	8.4	17.9	14.2
International development institutions	1.1	1.1	0.9	0.3	—	1.6	2.5
Total	$98.2	$98.2	$67.2	$60.3	$52.4	$91.7	$125.6
Memorandum item: LDC borrowing excluding "managed" loans[b]	$40.5	$17.9	$11.8	$ 9.3	$11.9	$10.5	$ 10.3

SOURCE: Organization for Economic Cooperation and Development, *Financial Market Trends* (March 1985, May 1989).
a. All amounts are in billions of U.S. dollars.
b. New money in the form of syndicated credits provided under the umbrella of rescheduling packages. It is worth noting that the average spread on loans to LDCs has dropped from 92 basis points in 1985 to 57 basis points in 1988. A basis point is 1/100 of a percent.
NOTE: The table covers the aggregate of foreign bank credits and medium-term bank loans, excluding commitments classified as "other international bank facilities."

fail to increase capital or better monitor their own risks, [the Fed] may move to more formal regulation of capital levels."[5]

By the close of 1986 U.S. and U.K. regulators finalized an accord that formally established higher base-capital levels for regulated banks and brought off–balance-sheet exposures onto the balance sheet in accordance with a risk-weighting scheme. This affected interest-rate and currency swaps, note facilities of all types, options and futures, bankers' acceptances, forwards, contingent credit guarantees, and other products. Within twelve months the U.S./U.K. accord was negotiated and eventually adopted by the central banking authorities in OECD countries. It stands as a landmark achievement of international coordination in banking regulation and addresses a widespread concern about the weakening of internal banking controls.

New products are examined in detail in chapter 2. A summary of principal products is given below.

[5]*International Financing Review* (London; IFR) (April 27, 1985): 58

Interest-Rate Swaps

An interest-rate swap occurs when two parties have different funding needs and capabilities. If the first party has access to cheap fixed-rate funding in deutsche marks, and the second party has access to cheap floating-rate finance in U.S. dollars, then each may borrow and contract to exchange interest payments with the other. Sometimes, the bank that arranges these deals serves as collector or guarantor of the transaction and assumes a contingent liability. Interest-rate swaps often have a cross-border dimension, where one leg of the swap is based in a low-interest-rate country like Japan and the other in a higher-rate country.

Prior to regulatory intervention, the interest-rate swap market grew from an estimated $3 billion in 1982 to around $80 billion in 1984. This explosive expansion was nearly all off the balance sheet and thus was not reflected in banks' capital bases or included, for the most part, in institutional controls on counter-party and country exposure.

Loan Swaps and Loan Sales

One outcome of the debt crisis has been the effort to liquidate or trade out of exposures to problem debtor countries. Such swaps occur for a variety of reasons including, on the part of U.S. banks, the desire to avoid disclosure requirements when more than 1 percent of total assets are concentrated in one country, to better regionalize portfolios, and to reduce the book value of loans taken by a local subsidiary of a multinational company (MNC). Loan swaps and sales have become so common over the last few years and have affected so many different kinds of credits that the activity has begun to resemble an adjunct to segments of the bond market.

Note Facilities

Whether they take the form of note-issuance facilities, Euro-notes, Eurocommercial paper, or some other variant, the banks that back note facilities make a medium-term commitment of credit on the strength of the borrower's short-term negotiable paper. Prior to regulatory intervention, note facilities were by and large off the balance sheet. Furthermore, competitive pressures once forced banks to compete aggressively on price, creating downward price spirals that virtually guaranteed that risks were not being properly evaluated—a source of worry to U.S. and U.K. regulators who cite such facilities as one phenomenon that prompted them to stiffen capital-adequacy regulations.

Multi-Option Facilities

Multi-option facilities (MOFs) are specially structured facilities that allow the borrower access to different markets and currencies through a number of linked programs.

> The main characteristic of multiple component facilities is to provide a borrower with the possibility of using different financing instruments according to his specific requirements at a given moment and to funding availability and cost on various market compartments. These facilities typically incorporate a number of options for borrowing in a variety of currencies and maturities, such as note placements, usually through a tender panel, short-term bank advances, revolving stand-bys, and swingline facilities to support Euronote or commercial paper facilities.[6]

These and other new financial instruments have made risk evaluation more difficult. They can weaken traditional credit monitoring between bank and borrower or introduce lower-level credits into markets where assets are traded. They can be decomposed and packaged, at once increasing both the borrower's flexibility and the product's complexity. Many hinge on contingent future events and, at least initially, did not appear in conventional liabilities and assets. Indeed, given the pressures on bank capital, bankers tended to use contingent assets precisely because they did not show up on bank balance sheets.

[6] OECD, *Financial Market Trends,* (November 1986): 22.

Regulatory and Accounting Changes:
The United States

The increased fungibility of money and the permeability of national and offshore capital markets have prompted changes in the regulation and supervision of banks. Bank regulatory authorities have sought to discipline sovereign lending and more recently to scrutinize the consequences of financial innovation and the growth of off–balance-sheet banking.

Although new regulatory requirements on banks' international activity have increased dramatically over the past several years, in terms of both new behavior (such as provisioning and capitalization) and disclosure, banks have tended to provide as little information as possible. The new requirements therefore have imposed further and sometimes burdensome tasks on bank personnel.

These changes have directly and indirectly affected bank control functions, including the setting of lending limits and the analysis of risk. Recent regulation concerning the capital adequacy of banks has resulted in restrained asset growth both at home and abroad, which, in turn, has had contradictory effects. On the one hand, new regulations have reduced the need for all asset-generating parts of banks, including risk analysts, but the regulations have added to the burdens of country-risk analysts and bank officers assigned to rescheduling tasks.

In addition, bankers (particularly those in targeted institutions) have had to spend time and effort dealing with regulators, demonstrating their due diligence. Bank controllers have had to gather information about asset concentrations and to be sensitive to regulatory calculations of asset quality. Finally, bank regulators and supervisors have acted on their concerns about the extent and consequences of financial innovation and are beginning to mandate a series of changes in bank practices that are slowly but profoundly altering the job of the risk analyst. The remainder of this section outlines these changes.

Increased Disclosure to Shareholders

Banks are required by the Securities and Exchange Commission (SEC) to provide detailed information about lending activities and levels of exposure to various troubled sovereign borrowers. Regulations mandate that banks use an accounting guideline when preparing their financial statements. Specifically,

- According to SAB 49, banks must disclose to shareholders exposures equal to 1 percent of total outstandings to specified sovereign borrowers (¾ percent in certain cases).
- According to SAB 49(a), banks are required to report any payments problems related to loans to these sovereign borrowers—that is, the status of loans to countries currently restructuring or rescheduling their external debt.

These two guidelines reflect the regulatory influence of the SEC and, indirectly, the Financial Accounting Standards Board, which represents the accounting profession and acts as an unofficial supervisory authority whose disclosure guidelines are widely accepted.

Other Regulatory Controls

Parallelling SEC action, federal regulatory authorities (the Federal Deposit Insurance Corporation, Federal Reserve Board, and Office of the Comptroller of the Currency) and Congress now require banks to provide additional information about their international operations. The main relevant statutes are

- *The International Lending Supervision Act of 1983,* which requires banks to file Country Exposure Reports quarterly that provide a country-by-country breakdown of actual exposures exceeding 1 percent of total assets;
- *The International Lending Supervision Act of 1984,* which reiterates the reporting and disclosure requirements of the 1983 act and outlines accounting policies for various types of fees for international loans. Its objective is to eliminate the distorting

effects of such fees on banks' income statements by forcing them to amortize or spread fee income over the life of the loan.

Issues of Asset Quality

Public information is a powerful tool used by bank regulators and others to expose the lack of diversification in bank loan portfolios. The new disclosure requirements have played an important role in banks' decisions to all but stop lending to many sovereign borrowers.

However, disclosure also facilitated a crisis of confidence in the U.S. banking system, forcing regulators to establish and enforce new requirements to enhance the system's stability. Regulator concern over asset quality resulted in a set of new loan classifications—strong, moderately strong, other transfer-risk problems, substandard, value impaired, loss—as authorities attempted to balance two distinct goals:

- To reflect accurately the true status (and quality) of assets (i.e., performing and nonperforming) in banks' portfolios and encourage prudence in international lending practices;
- To create a mechanism for rewarding countries that adhere to International Monetary Fund austerity programs while rescheduling their foreign debt by allowing banks that lend to these countries to avoid setting up reserves against such loans.

These new classifications reflected areas of growing concern on the part of regulators and also directly affected bank behavior by mandating the setting aside of special sovereign loan-loss reserves for the lowest categories. Under the International Lending Supervision Act of 1984, banks are required to establish an allocated transfer-risk reserve (ATRR) for specified international assets. The federal banking authorities determine which international assets are subject to transfer risk, warrant establishment of an ATRR, the amount of the ATRR, and whether an ATRR may be reduced. The initial year's provision for the ATRR was 10 percent of the principal amount of the international asset.

Issues of Capital Adequacy

The ultimate issue with capital adequacy is the safety and soundness of the banking system. Because the last bulwark against loan losses is the banks' capital base, the real question is whether banks are adequately capitalized. Prior to the adoption of an international risk-based-capital rule in 1987, U.S. regulators had already increased the minimum capital to assets ratio from 5 percent to 5½ percent for large money-center banks.

Regulatory and Accounting Changes: Beyond the United States

Regulatory changes in the United States have been paralleled by changes in the major industrialized economies. In general, supervisory authorities have refrained from imposing official ceilings on the volume of new international lending by banks. The one notable exception is Japan, where the Ministry of Finance, for a period of time, mandated that the overall volume of Japanese banks' new international lending be limited to between 10 and 12 percent of the total syndicated loan market. Almost universally, these authorities have, in varying degrees, required greater and more frequent disclosure of banks' country and international exposures, both on an unconsolidated and a consolidated basis.

Attempts have been made to harmonize national bank regulation. Exchanges of information that were once intermittent and informal have become routine and formal. This has involved both the establishment and growing responsibility of various international supervisory groups, including the Committee on Banking Regulation and Supervisory Practices of the BIS, the Export Banking Group of the OECD, the Central Banking Department of the IMF, and the Groupe de Contact of the European Economic

Community (EEC). These groups have fostered a community of interest beyond national boundaries, which, in turn, has made it feasible for supervisory authorities to orchestrate some multilateral changes. The debt crisis and prominent bank failures (Ambrosiano, Schröder Münchmeyer) have led authorities to focus on a few key issues:

- A clearer definition of supervisory jurisdiction and responsibility and ultimately on who is the lender of last resort;
- Greater disclosure by banks of their foreign-exchange positions, country exposures, and liquidity positions (the disclosure of hidden reserves is still controversial);
- Consolidation of comparable financial data to accommodate the work of the international accounting associations to develop standardized accounting, audit, and disclosure principles and practices for multinational banking.

These groups also recommend establishing international prudential policies on banks' maturity transformation (converting a short-term facility into a long-term facility), capital adequacy, lending limits, bad-debt allocations, and nonperforming loans.

Contingencies: The Balance Sheet behind the Balance Sheet

In 1985 a new round of regulatory actions and attendant publicity was directed toward the growth of off–balance-sheet banking. These contingent items frequently took, and still take, the form of back-up or stand-by facilities and therefore are viewed as being less risky than the direct extension of credit. Until drawn on, they do not involve the direct extension of credit, although banks generally have little control over when and whether a potential borrower may wish to actualize its lines. Because they did not appear on bank balance sheets in any way, they were not subject to various reserve and capital/prudential requirements.

The Extent of Off–Balance-Sheet Activity

The enormous sums involved are large enough to justify concerns about the balance sheet behind the balance sheet. In grappling with this issue, regulators examined a largely overlooked source of actual profits and potential credit commitments.

Table 1.3 presents data from the end of the first quarter in 1985, precisely the time that regulatory debate in the United States (within the Federal Reserve Bank and the Office of the Comptroller of the Currency) and the United Kingdom (largely confined to the Bank of England) began to intensify. The table comprises

TABLE 1.3

Commitments and Contingencies

Bank[a]	Commitments and Contingent Liabilities[b]	Total Recorded Assets[b]	Contingencies as a Percentage of Total Assets
Citibank	$246.173	$122.492	201%
Bank of America	204.030	104.442	195
Chase Manhattan	144.043	79.810	180
Morgan Guaranty	103.513	63.364	163
Manufacturers Hanover	82.392	57.743	142
Chemical Bank	104.204	55.100	189
Bankers Trust	113.748	45.290	251
Security Pacific	42.573	39.147	108
First Chicago	74.542	35.901	208
Continental Illinois	26.058	28.478	91
Marine Midland	36.149	21.526	167
Wells Fargo	19.828	23.412	85
First Interstate	16.359	20.344	80

SOURCE: FFIEC 031 ("Call and Income Report"), Federal Financial Institutions Examination Council, made at close of business March 31, 1985, Schedules RC and RC-L.
a. These commitments and contingent liabilities are for U.S. banks only. They include items such as commitments to purchase and sell foreign exchange, when-issued securities, futures and forward contracts, stand-by and commercial letters of credit, and participations in bankers' acceptances. They are recorded in the form requested by federal banking authorities, thus at full nominal amounts, without netting and without distinction between drawn and undrawn facilities, both of which would substantially reduce the numbers shown. There are no line entries for interest-rate or currency swaps. Swaps, in particular, escape inclusion in this listing, which should be considered as a base amount and not a full amount. In its 1984 annual report, Morgan Guaranty discloses that its swap obligations equalled a notional principal amount of $11.2 billion; the amount at risk approximated $269 million as of December 31, 1984. At the time, Morgan Guaranty was unique among all the banks listed in disclosing this much information about its swap portfolio.
b. All amounts are in billions of U.S. dollars.

public information existing at the time and does not include all off–balance-sheet instruments. Thus, it does not reveal the full scope of the regulators' worries.

Causes of Off–Balance-Sheet Activity

The growth, to 1985, of off–balance-sheet items stems from a variety of sources, but one major impetus was increasing competition between commercial banks and investment and merchant banks. The large capital base of commercial banks gives them a key competitive advantage over others. They can create products (or do so in conjunction with investment banks) that through the provision of guarantees (that is, commitments and contingencies) lower the borrowing cost to issuers. Essentially, the money-center banks identified new areas of leverage.

The Regulatory Response: Risk-Based Capital Rules

Banks' ability to create new debt and avoid primary capital requirements was the primary impetus to the international regulatory effort that by 1988 produced an international set of standards known as risk-based capital rules. These standards imposed rules on the balance-sheet booking of contingencies and commitments, the composition of capital, and they raised the minimum acceptable level of the total capital base from what was a nearly universally acceptable 5½ percent of assets at book value to 8 percent of risk-weighted assets. Institutions are expected to meet a 7.25 percent ratio in 1990 and the full 8.0 percent ratio by 1992.

The risk-based capital rules represent the completion of a four-year process, but the release explaining the new rule indicated an agenda for the future:

> It should also be emphasized that capital adequacy as measured by the present framework, though important, is one of a number of factors to be taken into account when assessing the strength of banks. The framework in this document is mainly directed towards

assessing capital in relation to credit risk (the risk of counterparty failure) but other risks, notably interest rate risk and the investment risk on securities, need to be taken into account by supervisors in assessing overall capital adequacy. The Committee is examining possible approaches in relation to these risks. Furthermore, and more generally, capital ratios, judged in isolation, may provide a misleading guide to relative strength. Much also depends on the quality of a bank's assets and, importantly, the level of provisions a bank may be holding outside its capital against assets of doubtful value. Recognizing the close relationships between capital and provisions, the Committee will continue to monitor provisioning policies by banks in member countries and will seek to promote convergence of policies in this field as in other regulatory matters.[7]

The extent to which the present spirit of cooperation will endure and further progress be made, especially in a period of intensified acrimony over trade in financial services, is very much an open question.

[7]Bank for International Settlements, *International Convergence of Capital Measurement and Capital Standards* (Basle: BIS Committee on Banking Regulations and Supervisory Practices, July 1988, BS/88/62e), p. 3.

2

The Risks, the Products, and the Controls

In no sense do banking institutions make full disclosure of their risk controls systems and techniques. Nor, necessarily, should they. One difference between banking today and banking ten or even five years ago is that a fairly staid sideline activity has moved center stage. The ability to control risks now enters into decisions about funding, product development, marketing, and information systems. It may determine future success or failure in the industry—especially if, as some expect, those who best control risks also are the lowest-cost producers of financial services over the medium and long terms.

What disturbs some observers, however, is the feeling that banks may not fully disclose their practices to the regulatory authorities. Frequent conversations over the years with those from both sides have convinced us that disclosure does not routinely occur at the examiner's "street-level" view (nor would the field examiner necessarily be prepared to fully appreciate what was disclosed) and that it may not be as common as generally supposed at the higher levels of dialogue. One supervisory official complained in a recent interview, "Risk assessment should be consolidated at the top of each institution. This is a problem in the relations between the regulators and banks. Regulators deal with divisions in the institution within their purview, such as broker/dealers, but not the entire organization."[1]

In short, the timing and contents of disclosure may depend on what the public regulatory official knows to ask about, but this in turn tends to be functionally splintered—between the bank and and the regulator. As one former regulator, now working on Wall Street, has observed, "The only advantage regulators have over other people is that of collective knowledge. They can spot anomalies from one institution to another, but little more than this."[2] This lack of transparency permits a potentially hazardous element of blindman's bluff to pervade the industry–regulatory agency relationship.

The New Risks

The new products can be categorized according to five types of risk: credit, price, market liquidity, country, and settlement.

Credit Risk

Credit risk materializes when a contracting party fails to perform as specified, causing a financial loss. Credit failures typically arise from instances of bankruptcy, supervening legislation, and other legal events.

A number of the new products involve minimal credit risk, at least compared with their nominal amounts. These instruments—such as swaps, forward-rate agreements, futures, and options—hedge the effect of price fluctuations or convert one kind of price risk into another. The interest-rate swap, for example, transforms the interest rate of a borrower's obligations. Actual credit exposure is small, by industry consensus amounting to less than 3 to 4 percent per annum of the swap's face amount. The risk-reducing properties of products that do

---

[1]Multinational Strategies interview, 1988.
[2]MNS interview, 1988.

carry credit risk have tended to either shorten the term of the credit exposure, theoretically lowering the holder's risk, or securitize the risks through the obligations of high-credit-quality borrowers.

Securitization

For most mortgage-backed securities, a good example of a securitized credit, the credit risk on the securities equals that of the pool of underlying obligations—in this case, the mortgages. Given the high credit performance of most home mortgages, the quality of the security is equally high. In the case of lower-quality mortgage obligations, a credit booster, often in the form of a contingent letter of credit insuring a portion of the credit, may be employed. Such techniques effectively parcel out the credit risk, passing a substantial portion to the issuer of the contingent guarantee.

Shortened Exposure

Note-issuance facilities (NIFs) are representative of a class of instruments that modify risk by shortening the term of the credit exposure. The facility itself, which can endure from one to fifteen years, represents a medium- or long-term commitment, but the credit exposure is linked to periodically issued notes that are money-market instruments maturing in thirty to ninety days of issue. The issuing bank's term commitment to the facility represents as much market-liquidity risk as credit risk. The standard NIF contract requires issuing and tender panel banks to provide access to the market or funds only on condition that the financial standing of the borrower does not deteriorate materially. Of course, whether these covenants will function as designed in times of serious financial market stress remains to be seen. A substantial number of NIFs are, from the outset, not drawn and are used only as back-up lines to improve the liquidity of the borrower. In these cases, commitment and credit risks remain contingent until activated.

Price Risk

Price risk is the risk that an instrument's market value will fall in direct or indirect connection with fluctuations in other financial prices. It is the risk of an adverse move in market value, considered separately from other risks.

Many new instruments have the capacity to unbundle or separate price risk from credit risk on the principal amount of a particular transaction. Unpacking risks in this way is a genuine novelty and a particularly attractive feature of the new products. The variation in the way each new instrument structures price and credit risk allows a user considerable flexibility and potential precision in managing a financial portfolio.

With flexibility, however, comes significantly greater instability in the prices of financial instruments. Only a few years after the Nixon administration removed the United States from the Bretton Woods system, inaugurating the era of floating exchange rates, financial analysts and commentators began to notice structural shifts in the organization and behavior of investors in the capital markets.

In 1981 Martin Liebowitz of Salomon Brothers observed the demise of the traditionally passive, coupon-clipping bond investor—the proverbial Belgian dentist—in favor of more active opportunists:

> A prime characteristic of these new bond market investors is their heterogeneity. Another is their elusiveness and the discontinuity that this engenders in the market place. The new classes of investors become active for their own reasons, have an interest in specific types of securities, and even then only at times that suit their needs. There is very little of the continuous flows from ready investors that gave the bond market its old depth and resiliency.[3]

Product innovations that segregate price from other kinds of risks have been contemporaneous with and may aggravate extraordinary price lurches in the capital markets. In a recent survey, analysts performed calculations of security price volatility and the volatility of price volatility (defined as the standard devi-

[3]Martin Liebowitz, *Vistas for Innovation* (Salomon Brothers, November 1981), p. 3.

ation of rolling twenty-day volatility divided by its mean), comparing the track records over two time periods for U.S. treasury bond yields and stock prices.[4]

For the periods 1980–82 and calendar 1987, the calculations indicated that price changes (volatility per se) have not grown more extreme but the frequency of change within any given short-term period (the volatility of volatility) has sharply escalated. For bond yields the volatility of volatility in 1987 was 42.4 percent compared with 24.3 percent in 1980–82; for stock prices as measured by the S&P 500 index the respective figures were 86.1 percent compared with 27.5 percent. Price volatility in this brave new world is not inherently undesirable. Participants in the financial markets have a vital and legitimate interest in some degree of volatility, which gives rise to profit opportunities. But the new products in their price risk-transforming behavior pass substantial risk from counterparty to counterparty.

Market-Liquidity Risk

Market-liquidity risk is a typically short-term absence of buyers that either precludes the immediate sale of an asset at its full value or greatly restricts the volume that can be sold at full value. *Short term,* as a term of convenience, may extend from days to months.

Of all the risks engendered by new financial products, this may prove to be the most pernicious. Pioneering financial innovations are traded in new markets that, in many cases, have not been tested by full interest-rate or business cycles, or when tested have shown a disturbing tendency to stop functioning. These seizures have affected instruments traded within organized exchanges (which, in theory and generally in practice, promote orderly trading conditions through improved disclosure and self-regulated trading practices) and those traded outside exchange structures directly between institutions.

The following three notable disruptions occurred without being prompted by a shiver in a larger, more important credit market and were largely isolated from most other markets. Their

[4]*Prospects for Financial Markets in 1988* (Salomon Brothers, December 1987), p. 5.

liquidity problems, however, demonstrate the degree to which problems can be precipitated by unsuspected causes and can adversely affect the credit of large, integrated, and international participants that also participate in other markets.

Floating-Rate Notes

The perpetual floating-rate note market (FRN), which is an over-the-counter, essentially interbank market, congealed with amazing rapidity in late 1986 when the six principal London-based market makers decided to cease swapping paper among themselves. In that case Japanese bank investors were left holding the largest portion of resultant book losses on suddenly illiquid securities. As table 2.1 shows, new issues in the *entire* floating-rate note market (not merely the perpetual segment) rapidly dropped off in 1987.

The London Metals Exchange

The tin crisis of 1986, which took place within the context of the London Metals Exchange (LME), occurred when the international tin agreement (and prices) failed by virtue of a bankrupt price-support fund. The subsequent confusion lightened the pockets of a number of LME participants by an estimated 600 million pounds.

The Commodities Exchange

After the Commodities Exchange (COMEX) crisis of 1985, which hinged on the bankruptcy of three COMEX members, remaining

TABLE 2.1

Illiquidity in Floating-Rate Notes

	1984	1985	1986	1987	1988
As percentage of total new financings	19.4%	20.9%	13.1%	3.3%	4.9%
Total[a]	$17.36	$58.71	$51.03	$12.96	$22.12

SOURCE: Figures adapted from OECD *Financial Market Trends*, 1985–89.
a. In billions of U.S. dollars.

members of the exchange needed a full six months to sort out the obligations to other participants in the gold options market.

Country Risk

Country risk has conventionally been defined as the risk that a public- or private-sector entity will become unable to fulfill cross-border financial obligations. More specifically, it is the risk that a given sovereign will find itself unable or unwilling to service these obligations because of a shortage of foreign exchange.

Traditional country risk applies equally to all the new products that require payments in foreign currency, a quality that characterizes most new products at least some of the time when they are applied in foreign-currency areas. It particularly applies to products that extend credit.

To accept only this traditional banker's definition of country risk, however, ignores the broader, evolving risk implications of doing business with new products and services on a global basis. While that definition is useful because of its clarity and specificity, we should keep in mind a much wider—although vaguer— interpretation. We should consider country risk also as the risk to the successful completion of a transaction arising out of the divergent behavior, systems, or legal culture of a foreign national context.

Comparing securities with traditional loans in a 1985 interview, the credit chief for a major New York money-center bank captured this viewpoint: "Occasionally the capital markets people will come to me with a deal where they propose that it has no country risk at all. . . . For example, some French bonds, which you know you can always sell—the question is at what price. There they would claim to have converted all the country risk into market risk. We have never agreed with that viewpoint. . . . As long as you are exposed to that country, you have country risk."[5]

Consider the case of a fund manager who wants to liquidate a book gain in a major Italian company's equity shares and issues the trade order. The sale occurs, but the manager fails to collect

[5]MNS interview, 1985.

because delayed and unsettled prior trades clog the domestic exchange's clearing facilities. Besides losing the use of the fund's money for weeks or even longer, the manager also may find that getting the trade cleared requires the payment of a little vigorish to a local agent. This too is country risk in one of its more recent guises—that of settlement risk.

Settlement Risk

Settlement risk is the very short-term danger that a trade will fail to be completed—for reasons such as bankruptcy of a counterparty or technical processing problems—in the brief period between the trade date and the trade settlement date. Conventionally, the danger is that one party will deliver securities to the other without receiving prompt payment. The risk is cumulative: the greater the number of counterparties to a transaction, the more probable a settlement hitch will occur.

A former chairman of Morgan Guaranty, Robert Lindsay, spoke for many in banking when he said in a 1987 interview, "Some people, and I'm among them, are concerned that the next major problem to hit banking will not involve the concerns of today, like energy, real estate and overseas lending. The major problem will be a combination of a credit failure and a systems failure, which will lead to a loss of confidence in the markets."[6]

Systems Failure: The Milan Bourse

In late 1987 and early 1988 the systems-related operation delays and snags experienced in several markets proved Lindsay prophetic on the question of systems failures. Fortunately, systems overload and breakdown did not combine with a significant negative credit event, but for the first time operations risk for both new and conventional instruments drew widespread attention.

The principal Italian exchange in Milan is one frequently cited example of systems failure. The Milan bourse was a financial backwater until 1985, but changes in law permitting the creation

[6]William W. Streeter, "What Banking's Coming To," *ABA Banking Journal* (March 1987): 29.

of local mutual funds rechanneled money flows in the domestic economy. Within twelve months, the stockmarket index had doubled, and by late 1987 the market's reputation had toppled.

Some fund managers (James Capel Co. of London being prominent among them) withdrew from the market altogether. A complaint voiced by another manager at the time expresses general industry frustration: "There was no way of knowing where the money was—we had more than $100 million there at the peak— or the status of any trade or the location of securities. . . . We pulled out completely. To get out fast, we had to offer a bribe to the bank for cash settlement; we paid a 1 percent discount on the value of the securities."[7] The consoling rationalization that this typified only some European exchanges, already notorious for sluggish back offices, was exploded less than six months later when large backlogs of unsettled trades developed in London.

Volume Effects

As communications and processing facilities have improved, and processing-related trade transaction costs have decreased, the volume of financial transactions has increased by exponential amounts. The base of collected funds against which transactions of all sorts are cleared also has increased, but at a comparatively modest rate.

The possibility of something going wrong in the back office has drawn front-office attention to cost effects, which can pile up quickly and unexpectedly. The magnitude of what might go wrong can be gauged only impressionistically. When a rare computer failure at the Bank of New York, a bank with a sizable but not unique clearing business, occurred in 1986, the bank had to borrow $22.6 billion from the Federal Reserve to meet its obligations until the system could be restored. Machine error is only one manifestation of operation risk, especially in a world where most securities markets use physical delivery rather than book-entry clearing systems.

[7]Larry Marion, "The Securities Clearing Time Bomb," *Institutional Investor* (April 1987): 239–42.

The Products

Using the above definitions, this section examines the risks attending key generic new-product transactions.

Note-Issuance Facilities and Other Note Facilities

Salomon Brothers offered a comprehensive definition of a note-issuance–type facility in late 1985, when the product was extremely popular:

> A note issuance facility is a generic term for a syndicated financing arrangement that guarantees an issuer access to a certain amount of funds for a prescribed length of time. At any time during the term of the facility, the borrower may request a portion of the facility by drawing down, which results in an offering of short-term securities. These negotiable instruments are evidenced by promissory notes and are usually brought to the market for periods of one, three or six months. At the end of each interest period, notes may be repaid or offered in a new tranche. Notes are offered through a sole dealership or an auction mechanism to short-term investors. If an issuer's full request is not purchased by these investors, the notes are sold to a group of underwriting banks who commit, in advance, to purchase the notes at a predetermined spread, which is generally relative to LIBOR. Alternatively, these underwriting banks may provide funds through a separate lending arrangement.[8]

There have been many variants on the NIF concept (producing a slew of acronyms), including RUFs (revolving underwriting facilities), TRUFs (transferable underwriting facilities), STUFs (short-term underwriting facilities), STIFs (short-term issuance facilities), SNIFs (short-term note-issuance facilities), and others. All products in this generic category share impor-

[8]Gioia M. Parente, *An Introduction to Note Issuance Facilities* (Salomon Brothers Bond Market Research, 1985), p. 1.

tant advantages. For the borrower they can shave funding costs—if needed immediately—or cheaply provide back-up liquidity. For banks the advantages are no longer as compelling, but until recent regulatory changes, the facility could be signed, a fee received, and no asset recorded on the balance sheet until or unless the facility was drawn on. It was quintessential off–balance-sheet business that produced income now, incurred no reserve costs, created no balance-sheet impact, and represented a contingent rather than actual commitment.

Associated Risks

The risks incurred with NIFs vary by facility. The contingent underwriting commitment creates a credit risk that is closely analogous to that of a revolving loan. The bank is obliged to acquire an asset at the behest of the borrower. This is essentially true for the lead dealer bank. Institutions that take part in a tender panel can choose whether or not to bid for notes.

The most worrisome risk aspects of these instruments, at least for regulatory authorities, tend to be (1) their "hidden" quality as off–balance-sheet contingent items; (2) their easily mimicked structure, which allows fierce price-cutting competition to develop swiftly, causing worries of underpriced risk when the facilities are increasingly marketed to lower-grade borrowers; and (3) the degree to which, in the market's early days, borrowers and potential lenders misunderstood each other. Market practice is now much more consistent, but as recently as 1986 virtual contradictions were enshrined in contract language regarding the user's right to draw on and the bank's obligation to back the facility. More specifically, during the mid-1980s NIFs were signed where the lender inserted convenants preventing utilization in case of "material change" in the borrower's creditworthiness, yet the borrower wrote among the conditions for utilization the instances of constricted cash flow and illiquidity that might well be construed as material changes.

Unlike the ultimate investors, note holders acquire a familiar money-market risk. They purchase a short-term asset whose interest rate is fixed and thus incur price risk equivalent to that of assets of comparable maturity.

Currency Swaps

As a product, the currency swap is older than the interest-rate swap, although it has been overtaken by the latter in terms of market size. In a currency swap, two firms agree to sell each other currency over time with a commitment to reexchange the principal amount of currency at maturity. Normally, but not always, fixed interest rates are used in each currency. Figure 2.1 shows company A selling $20 million to company B in exchange for just over £11.74 million at current exchange rates. Both pay common reference rates of interest on the financing received. A pays 15 percent per annum, probably in semi-annual payments, while B pays 8⁹/₁₆ to A, also probably in semi-annual payments. At maturity the principal amounts are swapped back.

Associated Risks

Both price and credit risk are present in swap transactions. Matching or hedging swap positions can eliminate all or most price risk but does not reduce an intermediary's exposure to credit risk. An intermediary's credit exposure depends on the joint probability of an adverse move in interest rates and a performance failure by the swap counterparty. The credit exposure on a swap is the potential loss when a counterparty fails. The magnitude of this loss, which is determined by the market value of the

FIGURE 2.1

Basic Currency Swap

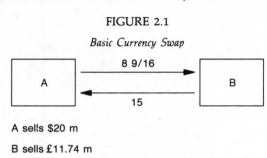

A sells $20 m

B sells £11.74 m

swap contract at current interest rates, is limited to the cost of reestablishing the swap's interest and currency flows at current market rates.

When a swap transaction involves an exchange of currencies delivered to locations at different times or in different time zones, the swap party is exposed to settlement risk. This exposure arises when one party has fulfilled the obligation under the contract by delivering funds but does not receive the offsetting funds from the counterparty. Most intermediaries attempt to minimize settlement risk by matching the timing of each set of payments as closely as possible.

Interest-Rate Swaps

For borrowers, the beauty of interest-rate swaps is simple. Consider the World Bank's experience with lower-cost funding achieved through interest-rate swaps. As one of the first and most aggressive promoters of the swap market for its own funding needs, the Bank has had more experience with these instruments than almost any other borrower. The Bank stated that in 1983 swaps lowered its average cost of borrowing from about 10 percent to 8.9 percent. In the second half of 1986 it reported that average rates had been cut from 6.6 percent to 5.77 percent. Many, if not the majority, of its borrowings now have a swap associated with the basic borrowing. SEK, the state-controlled Swedish Export Credit agency, reported that at the end of 1985 it had managed, through active use of swaps on the Euromarket, to fund itself at an average of one full percentage point below LIBOR during that year.[9]

There are other key advantages of an interest-rate swap:

- It does not involve any exchange of principal amounts;
- The number of market participants is large;
- The market mechanics, once a sore spot, have been standardized—allowing deals to be done quickly and lowering some elements of risk arising from unfamiliar documentation.

[9]Peter Montagnon, "How SEK Funds at One Point below LIBOR," *Financial Times,* Dec. 9, 1985, p. 27.

In its simplest early form, the interest-rate swap was designed to take advantage of an arbitrage between the credit-quality standards of the fixed-rate bond market and the floating-rate, short-term (usually bank loan) market. The arbitrage was premised on differing perceptions of the relative advantages of a strong credit (AAA) and a less strong credit (say, a single B).

A common situation might see B borrowing at LIBOR (London interbank offered rate) plus .5 percent from its bank in the form of a revolving-loan facility with a three-year term (see figure 2.2). Counterparty AAA, if it were to fund itself by borrowing from its bank on a short-term basis, would probably pay an interest cost of LIBOR plus .25 percent, whereas if it funded itself through a ten-year bond, its interest cost would be LIBOR plus .5 percent. B, by contrast, may not be able to borrow readily in the bond market or, if it does borrow, pays about 200 basis points (2 percent) more for its funds than AAA. Thus there is a substantial funding difference between the two firms.

Assume that LIBOR is 10 percent. In a simple swap an investment or commercial bank arranges for AAA to issue a ten-year bond paying 11 percent. B borrows short term at LIBOR plus .5 percent, or 10.5 percent. The intermediary bank would pay AAA's 11 percent coupon and in return would receive from B 11.25 percent, 11 percent of which is used to pay the coupon for AAA. AAA in turn pays the bank LIBOR, or 10 percent, which it, in turn, remits to B.

FIGURE 2.2

Basic Interest-Rate Swap

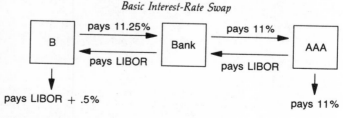

LIBOR = 10%
B gets 10-year money at 11.75%, saving .25%

Bank gets .25%
AAA gets 10-year money at LIBOR, savings 1%

Everyone gains. B gets ten-year money (rather than three-year funds) at a total cost of 11.75 percent, at least 25 basis points under what its cost would be for a ten-year borrowing. AAA gets ten-year money at the LIBOR rate of 10 percent, thus saving 100 basis points; and the bank gets an intermediary's fee of 25 basis points.

Associated Risks

These simple examples only roughly resemble the complex, multiple-counterparty interest-rate swap transactions that have evolved. The nature of the role played and resulting risks faced by intermediary banks in swap transactions has not changed as much.

A material credit risk is represented by counterparty B, and this is assumed in the transaction. A number of intermediary roles exist. A bank can act merely as middleman by introducing two compatible counterparties and backing away once the agreement has been signed. This "laying off" of a swap is especially characteristic of investment banks, which, at least in the market's early days, had neither the capital nor the inclination to develop a portfolio reflecting their views on interest or exchange rates. A bank can act as collecting agent, staying with the swap throughout its life and accepting some level of risk (such as delayed payment). Banks, and commercial banks in particular, also serve as guarantors. As such they guarantee the credit of one counterparty, or are themselves the counterparty, offsetting one swap against another with a second counterparty.

The credit risk faced by an intermediary bank arises from two sources: counterparty failure and interest-rate risk over the life of the swap. If interest rates move in the wrong direction but the counterparty does not fail, there is no problem. Equally, if the counterparty fails but interest rates move in favor of the bank, then it may find that the bankruptcy of its counterparty crystallizes a profit rather than a loss. (It should be noted here that the swap market, unlike that for many new instruments, has matured into a highly liquid market with active, global, corporate participation; replacement costs, therefore, tend to be low.) The stan-

dard conclusion is that risk will materialize only if the counterparty fails and interest rates move in the wrong direction. This
is essentially correct but fails to do justice to some worrisome
aspects of the market.

The more risk a counterparty credit poses, the more likely it is
that the intermediary bank will be drawn into the swap as collector, guarantor, or counterparty. Against the danger of credit risk,
many commercial bankers will protest that you do swap business
only with companies with credit and operations well known to
the bank. That is often true. Its truth, however, does not change
the facts that (1) at competitive moments in the past, swap
originators have reached down in the credit tiers for low or less-
than-investment-grade counterparties and (2) the commoditiza-
tion of the swap business is having that effect again today.

For example, many of the swaps concluded in 1983 and 1984
had U.S. savings and loan associations (S&Ls) as counterparties.
Not only was this a troubled and weakened industry during
that period (much less now), but these counterparties were not
all first- or even second-tier credits. In 1983 many S&Ls
swapped into fixed-rate liabilities to match their fixed-rate assets. In these swaps, they paid floating-rate money to receive
fixed. Between January and May 1984 interest rates rose. This
made these contracts profitable: they were paying out a fixed-
rate sum lower than the floating-rate obligations their counterparties had taken on. Many S&Ls cashed in on the swaps and
risked returning to floating-rate liabilities, thereby mismatching
their books. Fortunately rates moved downward in May so the
S&Ls could rehedge at lower rates. This is an example of arbi-
traging through swaps that was successful but might well not
have been.

Risk at the System Level

A second source of potential risk is more systemic and virtually
unexplored. In 1981 and 1982, when swaps were novelties, interest-rate swaps involved few counterparties. From 1981, when the
face value of all swaps concluded amounted to no more than $1

billion, to mid-1987, when commercial banks signed $521 billion worth of agreements, the entire complexion of the market changed.[10] As one former regulator put it, "It is much more difficult to know where your risks are. . . . When you have counterparties to counterparties to counterparties, et cetera, where does the chain end? Sure, you can bring a problem into the courts, and you'll probably recover your claims, but not for several years. Besides, sometimes it is unclear what jurisdiction the claim will fall under."[11]

Swaps are no longer the completely untested products they were in the mid-1980s. Based on an informal survey we suspect that nearly every major New York money-center bank and a few investment banks have suffered at least one counterparty default without incurring a significant loss. Defaults have occurred when transactions were profitable and, in a very liquid market, could be reset. They have occurred when the credit of the defaulting counterparty was backed by another institution's letter of credit or satisfactory collateral. Even the much improved swap documentation found in today's agreements has not yet been tested in court.

Although actual measurement of the risk amount can vary widely among market participants, consensus has emerged on the amount of credit risk involved in an interest-rate swap. A plausible worst-case scenario assumes that one's bank enters a deal with a counterparty that fails within a week, and that rates have moved unfavorably by 3 to 4 percent in the interim. On this basis, the implied credit risk is equivalent to 3 to 4 percent per annum on the face amount of the contract.[12]

Currency and Interest-Rate Options

An option is a contract between two parties that bind's one to allow the other to buy or sell an underlying instrument under specified conditions.

[10]"Institutional Investor," *Bank Letter,* April 18, 1988, p. 5.
[11]MNS interview, 1988.
[12]Julian Walmsley, *The New Financial Products* (New York: Wiley, 1988), p. 131.

Associated Risks

At least initially, currency and interest-rate options can be regarded as having two primary forms of risk: market risk and credit risk.

Options are unique in that both counterparties do not share the same price risk. The option writer sells a right and thereby creates a contingent liability that is potentially unlimited. For this the seller earns a fee (the premium). The buyer's price risk is limited to the premium paid for the option in the event that it expires without being exercised; conversely, the buyer's potential profit is limited only by the extent to which the current price of the underlying instrument moves past the strike price specified in the option contract.[13]

Extent of credit risk also differs between writer and buyer. The writer is at risk only for the amount of the premium owed by the buyer and only for a limited period of time between transaction and settlement. The buyer, on the other hand, is exposed to the writer for the full sum of the in-the-money amount—however large or small that may be—until the buyer exercises the option and settlement occurs. The subject of credit risk is complicated by the recent innovation of traded options, instruments that are no longer merely bought or sold but also traded over their contract life so that credit risk can pass from one intermediary to another. This is particularly true of options transacted outside official exchanges, over the counter, and between institutions.

Risk at the System Level

Once it becomes profitable to exercise an option, there are settlement risks to overcome. With foreign-currency options both the writer and the buyer are obliged to deliver one of the two currencies involved in the contract, regardless of whether the option is a put or a call (that is, whether it confers on the buyer the right to sell a currency at a given exchange rate against another currency or the right to buy the same). The exercise of an interest-

---

[13]A complete discussion of options can be found in Bank for International Settlements, *Recent Innovations in International Banking* (Basle: BIS, April 1986), pp. 61–120.

rate option requires the writer to either purchase or deliver underlying securities, while the buyer must produce either securities (a put) or cash for purchase (a call).

The respective sizes of official and over-the-counter markets can be gauged only roughly, but business is building quickly. By December 1987 the exchanges in London, Chicago, and Philadelphia reported 1.4 million outstanding interest-rate option contracts (three times the previous year's volume) and 805,000 outstanding currency options (an increase of 50 percent over the previous year). Estimates of over-the-counter interbank business indicate a daily turnover of $10 billion worth of currency options (notional face, not market-to-market) and $500 million of interest-rate options (again, face value).[14] A wide array of sophisticated option types has been created. A directory in the trade magazine *Risk* listed over fifty international banks offering close to seventy specific, over-the-counter option cocktails.

The volume of business and the lack of transparency especially evident in over-the-counter markets worry supervisory officials. Options essentially put a price on and then sell the volatility of whatever underlies the contract. They do not diminish risk but pass it to the portfolio of the final option writer. The options writer essentially insures (although the writer's risks are not necessarily diversified), which irks regulators who want to avoid cleaning up after a poorly made deal. The skills of the option writer therefore are of interest to writers, sellers, and regulatory officials.

Imbedded Options

Explicit currency and interest-rate options are sold as such either within exchanges or over the counter, but fixed-income instruments also include imbedded (i.e., built in) options. They often are difficult to identify and are transacted with incomplete understanding—on the basis of gut feelings mixed with a modicum of research. Experience with these instruments indicates two lessons:

[14]"Financial Brief: A Risky Business," *Economist,* May 28, 1988, p. 82.

- At the time of the transaction the hazards are either not seen or underappreciated;
- When seen, hazards tend to be underappreciated on the grounds that they are inconceivably remote; because the circumstances required for the realization of potential dangers have never occurred, the investor reasons that they will not occur.

The experience of sellers and investors with so-called heaven and hell bonds shows how quickly in today's markets the unthinkable can be realized.[15] A heaven and hell bond structure trades off the heaven that produces substantial up-front premium income for the investor willing to write an option for the hell that changes the conditions characterizing the underlying instrument on which the option is written and exposes the investor to substantial loss. The indexed currency-option note (ICON) was initiated in late 1985 and briefly flourished through 1986. The first ICON deal was arranged by Bankers Trust for the Long Term Credit Bank of Japan (LTCB), which issued ten-year dollar notes with a high coupon but a redemption price fixed at 169 yen to the dollar (the yen at that time was over 200 to the dollar). Any rise of the yen above 169 to the dollar correspondingly reduced the note's principal value. In this case a rate of 159 yen per dollar reduced principal to 94 percent; a spot rate of 84.5 yen per dollar eliminated principal value altogether.

The LTCB notes were bought mostly by other Japanese institutional investors who were, as one source characterized them at the time, "sitting on a pot of money and hungry for new investment material."[16] They could take comfort that for ten years the yen had never risen above 175 to the dollar and that the credit quality of the LTCB notes was unquestionably good. Although the market was illiquid at the time, the investment decision was not predicated on the possibility of trading out; this was considered a hold-to-maturity decision from the outset. In retrospect, this one proved risky. With the yen currently in a 130 to 145 trading range against the dollar (and dollar downside risk not

---

[15]This discussion draws on details presented in David Shirreff, "Caps and Options: The Dangerous New Protection Racket," *Euromoney* (March 1986): 26–40.
[16]MNS interview, 1987.

fully explored), those holding positions in this instrument have seen substantial principal value eliminated. Further, the instruments were underpriced and appeared to be seen as such even at the time. Given two bases for evaluating options pricing—the Black-Scholes technical model versus prevailing market rates—the model indicated the options required a much higher up-front premium than investors actually gained. One investment banker asked rhetorically at the time, "Are investors getting mugged or not? In the case of the Japanese it's not true. There is a massive savings ratio in Japan. The Japanese banks can swap [savers' low-cost deposits] for funds below LIBOR, and by investing at a yield above LIBOR can bear the risk of the option."

The comment is facile and only partially relevant. It ignores whether the issue was actually underpriced, answering instead the unasked question of whether Japanese investors could afford to bear the risk. More important, however, it ignores the progressive deregulation of deposit-rate ceilings in Japan—a deregulatory effort substantially pushed by foreign trade and monetary officials locked in fair trading practices negotiations with their Japanese counterparts. These deregulatory efforts have had a not inconsequential effect on cost of funds—especially when viewed against a ten-year, illiquid bet by the Japanese investing institution. Disaster has not materialized, but an investment decision made by a professional institutional investor on a short-term perception of risk in a little-understood instrument has materialized a loss of completely unexpected dimensions just three years down the road. Even among financial institutions with abilities to gather and analyze information far beyond those of the individual investor, clearly the quality of risk taking is not equal among all market participants.

Securitized Credits

Securitized assets are many and various. They include asset-backed securities (underlying assets commonly include mortgages, credit-card receivables, and auto loans), securitized bank loans of other types, junk bonds, and some types of note facilities. In the very broadest sense, securitization involves the substitution of the open markets for the loan markets, with a consequent dissolution or weakening of the ongoing credit relationship between bank and borrower. The securitization of credits shifts credit risk from the bank to investors, unless the former continues to guarantee the debt. The marketability of the securities increases the liquidity (as compared with credits) of investors without simultaneously reducing the liquidity of any other party. Securitized assets contain price risk equivalent to the risk that (in principal) existed on the underlying loans.

Mortgage-Backed Bonds

Mortgage-backed bonds constitute the best-known securitized asset. A mortgage-backed bond is a tradeable security whose cash flows rest on the cash flows of underlying home mortgages that usually have been segregated by prime characteristics (interest rate, maturity, credit quality) and pooled. The bond's effectiveness rests in erasing the distinguishing characteristics of single homeowners. Static credit—the individual home mortgage—becomes tradeable and therefore liquid.

The mortgage bond market has existed for twenty years or more on the strength of Ginnie Mae, Fannie Mae, and Freddie Mac pass-through or participation securities.[17] It has matured, however, only in the last six years with a series of innovations that first minimized prepayment risk (through collateralized mortgage obligations [CMOs] and real estate mortgage investment conduits [REMICs]), later unbundled the bonds' cash flows to compose diverse securities (interest-only bonds [IOs] and principal-only bonds [POs]), and finally permitted the tailoring of synthetic securities for specific institutional investors.

Most mortgage-backed bonds are of above-average credit quality both because of the U.S. homeowner's tendency to pay and because of federal government guarantees. With the latter,

[17]Ginnie Mae (GNMA or Government National Mortgage Association), Fannie Mae (FNMA or Federal National Mortgage Association), and Freddie Mac (FHLMC or Federal Home Loan Mortgage Association) provide a credit booster to qualifying home loans and securities backed by home loans. This federal government guarantee underpins the credit quality of the debt securities based on mortgages (pass-throughs) issued by these entities for funding purposes. Neither FNMA nor FHLMC provide a "full faith and credit" U.S. government guarantee, but both are U.S. government agencies and therefore are considered a near second-best in the market.

one deals with treasury bond credit quality while enjoying a significant increase in yield. The serious risks for investors are price related, particularly with the stripped IOs and POs, which are highly sensitive to changes in interest rates or related to the homeowner's free choice to prepay his mortgage at any time. Prepayment risk arises from the option imbedded in the common mortgage. As most homeowners know, if interest rates drop roughly 2 percent from the level on a conventional fixed-rate mortgage, they should refinance at the lower rate.

Early Market Phases. From the early 1970s to the early 1980s the market for mortgage-backed securities was limited because few investors wished, in effect, to write an interest-rate option in favor of the homeowner. Interest rates fall, the homeowner prepays, and the investor at the other end receives his money when he least wants it—at a time when market conditions will not allow him to reset his investment at an equivalent yield.

The market as it is currently configured took off in October 1981. As is so often the case, the trigger was not economic but political in nature. On September 30, 1981, Congress changed tax laws to favor U.S. savings and loans. The new rules did two important things. Any thrift that sold a mortgage loan at a loss would not have to take the full loss immediately but would be permitted to amortize the loss over the life of the sold loan. Better still, the thrift could apply its loss against taxes paid in previous tax years. The thrift industry was in trouble because of a prolonged interest-rate squeeze that resulted in funding costs higher than lending returns, so it moved quickly and in bulk, farming back taxes for profits. S&Ls were both the buyers and the sellers in this market, essentially marking their loans to market while buying the loans or mortgage-backed bonds already marked down and sold by other thrifts. All this activity was intermediated by a scarce handful of investment banks that briefly commanded monopoly trading fees and spreads.[18]

[18]Salomon Brothers dominated the market in its early period. Their traders went far beyond creating and trading mortgage-backed bonds to trading bulk volumes of mortgage loans with or without government credit support. In effect they bet the returns would outstrip any losses due to defaults on loans in their trading positions, and the bet turned out to be spectacularly correct. As Michael Lewis reports in *Liar's Poker* (New York: Norton,

Collateralized Mortgage Obligations.   The market found its second
wave with the creation of collateralized mortgage obligations
(CMOs). A CMO is a certificate entitling the owner to interest
payments from a pool of mortgages held in trust. The certificates
are divided into tranches, each with a different probability of
early repayment. The bondholder in the final tranche might not
avoid prepayment risk altogether but at least knows all the other
tranches will be liquidated first. Previously unanalyzed prepayment risk is separated into levels of probable risk (and therefore
implied maturities for the certificates).

Interest-Only Bonds, Principal-Only Bonds, and Synthetics.   CMO re-
finements came quickly. The first CMOs of three tranches gave
way to five- and then fifteen-tranche CMOs. Institutional investors became willing to enter the buy side of the market. As
investors' appetites for risk and novelty grew, CMOs spawned
interest-only and principal-only bonds (IOs and POs)—bonds
backed respectively by only mortgage interest payments and
mortgage principal payments.

Once the individual homeowner's interest payment was
definitively sliced from the principal payment, recombining the
two—creating synthetic securities—because the final CMO per-
mutation. In Michael Lewis's succinct description, "The 11 percent interest payment from condominium dwellers in California
could be glued to the principal payments from homeowners in a
Louisiana ghetto," thus tailoring a security to spec.[19]

Both IOs and POs are highly price sensitive to changes in
interest rates. Merrill Lynch stunned the market in early 1987
when it announced a $250 million loss on a single trader's posi-
tion in POs that could not be sold when their price plummeted
in a sudden fall of interest rates. This temporarily quieted innovation in the mortgage bond market, but by no means did it slow
the broader phenomenon of securitization. Temporarily blocked
in one direction, securitization moved sideways to encompass car

---

1989), p. 108, a single Salomon Brothers trader earned $100 million in 1984 trading whole
loans. Only Drexel Burnham's junk bond trading team rivaled (and surpassed) such feats
of money making.
[19]Lewis, *Liar's Poker,* p. 138.

loans, credit card receivables, and more. Other types of previously static credits became liquid.

Floating-Rate Notes

Floating-rate notes (FRNs) have been a mainstay of the Euromarkets for nearly two decades. The first Euromarket FRN was issued in 1970, and the first domestic U.S. FRN was issued by Citibank in 1974. Their popularity has tended to grow with interest-rate volatility because the note's principal value is comparatively stable compared to that of fixed-rate bonds. During the period from 1984 to 1986 the FRN market came under increasing competitive pressure from other, newly created instruments such as note-issuance facilities and interest-rate swaps coupled with fixed-rate bonds. The overall effect of this competition was to lower FRN pricing from a LIBOR base to LIMEAN (London interbank mean bid and offer rate) and subsequently LIBID (London interbank bid rate).

In liquid markets of high-quality name issues, this trend toward compression in pricing affected the market's profit dynamics but little else. It coincided, however, with the introduction of a variety of FRN structures that were never as liquid but that nonetheless were priced at equally low spreads. Key variations included perpetual floating-rate notes and, more generally, a whole sector of subordinated debt issued in FRN form.

Perpetual Floating-Rate Notes

For issuers, primarily banks, perpetual FRNs represent an attractive way of increasing primary capital without a rights issue that would dilute the equity base. The notes tend to be junior subordinated debt and are rated after outstanding debt but before common or preferred stock. Underlying the mid-1970s to mid-1980s boom in the issuance in perpetuals was the assumption that the notes would always be saleable at close to their issue price because interest would be periodically reset to current money-market rates and dealers would always stand ready to buy them back. Both assumptions proved incorrect.

During the second half of 1986 secondary-market trading amounts in perpetuals eroded noticeably, coinciding with a period of aggravated concern on the part of investors about the balance-sheet quality of the international banking sector as a whole. In November 1986 the market sector crashed. The bid side of the market disappeared, and the price of perpetual FRNs, on average, dropped a full 15 percent over the next five weeks. Trading essentially ceased. Market-making banks withdrew from their responsibility to make a market in these issues. Investors— in this case disproportionately represented by Japanese banks— were left holding substantial book losses.

Even though "perps" had been around for just over two years and elaborated on a familiar floating-rate concept, in retrospect it is clear that neither investors nor issuers fully understood the instruments that they were using. John Heimann, then vice chairman of Merrill Lynch capital markets, diagnosed the problem: "The market was confused over the difference between interest rate sensitivity and the value of liquidity. The market did not resolve the question as to whether the perpetual FRNs were capital market instruments or money market instruments. Once the market reached a consensus on these two points, market prices plummeted to compensate for the newly recognized increased risk level."[20]

Over succeeding months the contagion spread beyond perpetuals to affect all forms of subordinated FRNs, which also are largely issued by banks, although without the perpetuity feature. Dealers have steadily withdrawn from making a market since late 1987. The publication in early 1988 of regulatory proposals for an international unified risk-based capital rule (which implied that Japanese bank investors would have to deduct a proportion of their FRN holdings from their primary capital) sparked further public withdrawals in March 1988. Six dealers backed away, including J. P. Morgan, Union Bank of Switzerland, Fuji Bank, and Warburg Securities.[21] At the time only eleven dealers re-

[20]John Heimann, *International Capital Markets: Issues and Risks* (Paris: Institut d'Études Bancaires et Financières, 1987), p. 10.
[21]Stephen Fidler and Claire Pearson, "Six Dealers Drop Subordinated FRNS," *Financial Times,* March 15, 1988, p. 34.

mained active as market makers. Boom-and-bust market dynamics, proposed regulatory changes, and a growing investor concern over bank credit quality turned an apparently well-established Euromarket sector illiquid.

Leveraged Buyouts

Concomitantly with the merchant-banking strategy that has evolved among commercial-banking institutions, the international investment-banking population has begun to assume substantial credit risk and capital commitment. As the behavior of both classes of institutions converges, each moves closer to the other in terms of risks and business activities, and an uneven and incomplete kind of universal banking takes hold in major financial centers.

The most spectacular form of widespread capital commitment and credit-risk assumption found among both types of banking institutions is that of the leveraged buyout (LBO). An LBO traditionally has pulled commercial bankers and junk-bond investors together as lenders to a group of manager-investors who seek to purchase the entire equity of a target company. If successful, the equity is generally overwhelmed by the newly created debt, sometimes in a ratio as high as ten to one. The debt must be worked down as quickly as possible, usually off cash generated by asset stripping, or the company will fail to make good on the assumed interest payments. Most investment banks are late entrants to the game. They participate generally as the sole lender to manager-investors, offering enormous bridge loans and often committing the majority of the bank's capital, which must then be converted into bonds and placed.

Bridge loans, by their nature, are intended to last no more than three months or so. The nasty part comes if and when a bank fails to liquidate its position. It can happen to anyone, as Salomon Brothers discovered when a $275 million bridge loan to a small television broadcasting company, TVX, turned into a long-term equity position after two failed attempts to sell junk bonds to unwilling investors. It meant, as one competitor quipped, that to

Salomon's surprise, "It had joined the ranks of elite broadcast firms."[22]

Associated Risks

There are both risks to institutions and risks to the system in this kind of activity. First, and most obviously, a substantial credit risk is involved in assuming so concentrated a portion of a single company's obligations—obligations that are certain to overwhelm the company in the event that post-transaction plans do not work out. There is also market risk, as the Salomon anecdote points out. Investors might normally have purchased the planned participation of bonds except for bad publicity, an industry slump, and the final killer, Black Monday.

A further, relatively hidden credit risk ties in closely with these two and is particularly germane to investment banks. Distribution power is key to the investment banking business, present and future. The ability to place depends on relationships that are won over time and always subject to deterioration. Therefore, successful placing of a bridge loan may clean the bank's balance sheet, but unless it wants to spoil critical investor relations, the loan will carry with it the bank's tacit (and sometimes explicit) obligation to buy back what it sells at some reasonable price. During our interviews, more than one banker cited examples where a firm had been obliged to repurchase bridge-loan-related notes in the course of marketing yet another placement to the same investor population.

The point is not always widely understood, even in the banks themselves. One investment banking credit officer insisted that despite bridge financing, "As far as the [credit] term of our business is concerned, we're not extending our term but shortening it. Over the last few years we've shortened the overall term of our business to mostly six months or less. . . . In bridge financing you're in it for only one to three months."[23] Until the day arrives

[22]Elliott D. Lee, "Salomon Finds That There Are Pitfalls When Investing in Unfamiliar Markets," *Wall Street Journal*, June 14, 1988, p. 7.
[23]MNS interview, 1988.

when investment banks can afford to do without their investors, this is simply not true.

LBOs are nonetheless immensely popular because they carry fat arrangement and underwriting fees. LBO-related loans, precisely because of the risks, tend to pay somewhere between 150 and 200 basis points over the prime rate. But most important for both commercial and investment banks that end up as partial equity holders in a completed transaction, the returns can be as high as twenty times the equity invested.[24]

Investor awareness and risk concentration are troublesome questions at the systemic level. Who buys all those bridge loans, newly converted into bonds and notes? In most cases, the answer is other banks and near-banks: regional U.S. banks, second-tier European institutions, U.S. thrifts, Japanese banks (often not the well-known city banks). The pattern that begins to emerge is a familiar one: the passing and syndication of risk resembles the bum's rush of institutions into high-return syndicated sovereign lending in the 1970s.

One New York LBO fund manager commented, "Many believe that the next debt crisis will be in the LBO market. If there is a debt crisis, then the investment banks can exit the market. They would probably survive this. If there was a period of relative instability but not a concerted decay, then the investment banks would . . . find the buyers of their junk bonds who are also buyers of other products. These would be helped, but other [presumably smaller] buyers would not be."[25]

Caveat emptor.

Controlling the Risks

Market participants and regulators have reached consensus on at least one facet of the financial innovation risk question: all other things being equal, the innovations reduce risk for isolated insti-

[24]"America's Capital Markets Survey," *Economist*, June 11, 1988, pp. 9–10.
[25]MNS interview, 1988.

tutions precisely because of their risk-passing, risk-selling, risk-modifying qualities. Both groups are, however, more disturbed by innovation than if these changes had not appeared. Why? The key objections tend to come in two areas: (1) Are all other things equal—particularly in the sense of asking whether the new products are understood as well as the old? (2) Whatever the risk profile of single banking institutions, financial houses neither initiate nor carry out their affairs in isolation. The first point concerns us most here. From mid- to late 1985 institutions shared common perceptions about the risks that they and their competitors were engaged in and understood. Our 1989 survey revealed a striking degree of consensus, but the opinions have uniformly changed.

Perceived Risk

In late 1985 market participants and supervisory officials were concerned that few practitioners understood the risks entailed by the instruments and services they were offering. Senior managers and even some bankers originating new products worried especially that the credit department staff's function was being slowly, perhaps permanently, eroded by ever-accelerating innovation. In many cases, decisions reserved for credit officers and senior management might actually be made by juniors in the line and trading positions where so much product innovation was occurring.

Senior managers reacted by erecting a series of hastily designed organizational brakes. The product approvals process was formalized, and the level of senior approval required to do business was increased (but many worried that senior management might not understand the products being approved). Line people and traders were restricted to doing business with people included on carefully drawn lists of high-credit-quality entities. By late 1985 some banks were moving in the direction of intensive risk-exposure management of the new products on a facility-by-facility basis, apart from the established system of controls that covered each bank's routine activities. With this facility-intensive approach came the ascendancy of international czars backing up and overseeing the credit, and more broadly risk-control, side of the banks' activities in foreign markets. The goal, aptly summed up by a British banker, was "to put progressively higher hurdles in the path of line officers intent on doing bad business."[26]

Beneath the concern was an even sharper anxiety about just who was minding the store. According to one capital-markets specialist in New York, a veteran of many new product presentations, "Senior management doesn't understand them, the credit people generally don't grasp them, and the examiners tend to be the worst of all. . . . In fact we view our examinations as a teaching exercise."[27] Concerns at the Bank of England and the New York Federal Reserve tended to reflect this disquiet. Subsequent policy, particularly on the question of handling off–balance-sheet instruments, attacked the concern at its source by indirectly (through reserve requirements entailed by disclosing such instruments in the balance sheet) forcing higher prices for products and services.

Just under three years later the slower pace of innovation (sharply slower after the October 1987 crash) and an accelerated learning process on the credit side of most commercial banks have combined to enlarge the comfort zone shared by bankers and supervisors. One respondent expressed a widely held sentiment that "It is fortunate that [our] credit [department] has had a less challenging job in recent years. . . . If innovation were taking place today at the pace it did a few years ago, I'm afraid our systems would be hopelessly behind. We are catching up."[28] Another investment banking credit officer concurred: "It was in [the 1984 to 1985] period when we saw an enormous number of new products. I mean every day you would see a rash of 'whole-new-ballgame' things which you had to learn, had to understand, and had to evaluate. That has slowed down a lot, but it hasn't ceased."[29] In the Cross Committee report, discussed in detail later in this chapter, central bank supervisors articulated a cause for relief on the part of many bankers—the realization that despite

[26]MNS interview, 1985.
[27]MNS interview, 1985.
[28]MNS interview, 1988.
[29]MNS interview, 1988.

the proliferation of new names and add-ons, "New instruments unbundle the risks of traditional credit transactions, but the risks involved are in general the same."[30]

Contemporary worries, expressed most strongly by supervisory officials and somewhat less heatedly by the banking community, focus on questions of systemic risks: adequacy of control systems in aggregate, the lodging within the financial system of risk tied to options and futures contracts, and so forth. This shift in focus is a sign of real progress, implying a graduation in safety. It would, however, be reckless to conclude that all was well or that the tests of devices built by individual institutions for managing product-specific risks have been met and fully passed.

Improvements in Commercial-Bank Risk Controls

Commercial bankers have made progressively more sophisticated efforts to understand and manage the risks to which their institutions are exposed.

Credit-Equivalent Measures

Bankers proceed from their strength, which, above all else, is in understanding and controlling credit risk. The impetus therefore has been to understand and state as many forms of risk as possible in terms of credit questions and counterparty strengths. This can be seen in the nearly universal drive to reconcile conceptually divergent risks into integrated risk prices or credit-equivalent numbers. The bankers' temptation to swing at the fat pitch, then, has spawned methods with ingrained biases. Credit-equivalent numbers are very good at helping the organization distinguish between the people it wants to swap with and the people it doesn't, and at ballpark-pricing the risk. They are less good at gauging interest-rate risk, market-liquid-

[30]Bank for International Settlements, *Recent Innovations in International Banking*, p. 199.

ity risk, or the possibility of a settlement snafu with an unfamiliar traded asset.

Management Information Systems

Critical management information systems in money-center commercial banks are undergoing prolonged, expensive overhauls. If credit-equivalent numbers are used to systematically adjust for credit and price risks, all other questions must be resolved through less systematic experience and judgment. Without adequate and up-to-date information, many risk-related questions may not surface. Applying controls, once they have been decided, also requires significantly better, real-time MIS systems than most institutions currently can afford. Since 1986 most commercial banks have been caught in one of two positions: either out of date in terms of systems, in which case they rebuilt from scratch and now tend to lead the list, or caught somewhere between adequate and inadequate, with multiple divergent systems in need of overhaul, linkage, integration, and expensive new hardware and software applications.

Techniques of Portfolio Management

Banks use portfolio management to manage nontraditional exposures in increasingly sophisticated ways. Although the term's meaning can vary depending on situation and user, we use it to denote the shift toward more evolved, multitiered exposure limits systems as commercial banks rely less on a combination of credit limits (to control exposures to counterparties) and country limits (to monitor cross-border exposures). The senior credit officer of one bank clearly outlined the new layers of control:

> There are credit limits, which should be loans, off–balance-sheet items, or counterparties, all of which are brought down to a loan equivalent and brought through the credit system. Overlaying this, there are country limits and industry limits. Other limits come in under the broad area of market risk—market limits for individual

products, be it government securities trading, underwriting, equity trading out of London, FX trading. . . . There are limits for each of the disciplines and each of the activities.[31]

Portfolio management views increasingly large portions of the bank's balance sheet (and off–balance-sheet commitments) as liquid or nearly liquid. Installing limits controls and the necessary MIS back-up allows managers to quickly assess and monitor the risk positions that the bank may take as a result of its aggregate activity. In many institutions this has meant devising a discrete set of money market limits, trading limits, or underwriting limits (depending on the institution's terminology) and coordinating these with the existing MIS and limits-administration system. The process is often a long one. The progress that an institution makes can be measured by the extent to which (1) all bank activities fall inside the apparatus, (2) the merchant banking arm or in some cases subsidiary is incorporated and governed, and (3) the bank's (or bank holding company's) other recent acquisitions have been plugged in. Not everyone wants a complete grid. In some cases, decisions have been made to deliberately leave out new acquisitions. But everyone wants a more complete grid than they currently have.

Better Coverage

Incremental product inclusion has improved since the mid-1980s, and progress has been made in widening exposure limits systems to capture previously excluded activities. In late 1985 over half our sample of commercial banks did not incorporate interest-rate or currency-swap credit exposure under the credit limits, and few included foreign-exchange activity—whether spot or forward. Institutions debated the desirability of counting off–balance-sheet commitments like NIFs. Today all banks sampled (except for one laggard on currency swaps whose senior management cannot agree on what to measure the credit exposure at) count some portion of swap exposures under credit limits. Other off–balance-sheet commitments are counted, and all banks have

[31]MNS interview, 1988.

moved to capture significant portions of their foreign-exchange commitments within their in-house systems, although few have completely finished the job.

Applying the Controls

These general improvements in commercial bank-risk controls form the basis of the techniques and reforms governing business in specific product areas discussed in this section.

Interest-Rate and Currency Swaps

Interest-rate and currency swaps are good examples of how bankers' understanding of financial novelties has matured. By late 1985 investment banks were accustomed to swap products, and one London-based trading chief remarked how flat their profit dynamics had become. Between 1983 and 1985 his bank had seen fee income drop tenfold, while the volume of done swaps increased by a factor of three.

A new and more dangerous twist was introduced at that time by commercial bankers who put their money to work on the swap desk, accepting commitments as counterparties and building up multimarket, multicurrency swap books without quite knowing the amount of their credit risk, the adequacy of early documentation, and a host of other factors. The business was almost universally justified to us by respondents on the grounds that "after all, we do swaps only with our best customers, we don't do them that often, and they are vetted by senior management beforehand."[32] Subsequent research has shown that this was, perhaps, never entirely true. In any case, the swap business quickly became commoditized, substantial risk positions were built up, and better controls had to be devised.

Controls generally progressed from the inside out in organizational terms. Initial efforts concentrated on fitting the banks' own traders into a system of credit limits. Although some institutions have moved more slowly on currency swaps (not having the

[32]MNS interview, 1985.

benefit of Federal Reserve guidelines on credit risk) than on inter-est-rate swaps, consensus has been established on measuring the credit risk inherent in the latter. Dealers' associations—notably the International Swap Dealers' Association (ISDA) and the Brit-ish Bankers' Association (BBA)—standardized legal language and documentation for swap traders everywhere. Individual banks could then further their administrative controls by negotiating bilateral master agreements, which permitted better-drafted indi-vidual contracts to be struck with frequent counterparties. The establishment of credit-equivalent systems was pioneered by one or two banks and has become standard, permitting risk-return comparisons between deals to be made, an essential step in al-locating capital.

Currently industry efforts are focused on strengthening inter-nal management information: a real-time exposure count by product and counterparty is every institution's professed goal, and one or two in our sample have actually reached it. Most are somewhere in between. Despite high current levels of urgency, not all banks will carry through with their good intentions. The cost is high, and development efforts are full of frustration (wit-ness the number of banks that bought and discarded software systems they could not make work). Some managements will find that the expense of controlling some products outweighs the fee income to be won, but they will not necessarily choose to with-draw from the business.

Two aspects of risk have yet to receive much attention. The first is the problem of expanding the market, which is synony-mous with reaching down into lower and lower credit tiers to secure enticing returns. The relaxation of credit-rating barriers is a current reality at both commercial and investment banks, as institutions in both groups gingerly do business with below-investment-grade counterparties. A second problem concerns the increased number of transactions: no institution has successfully sized and accounted for this international web of swap linkages as a normal business risk in this sector. As a former senior U.S. regulator points out, the concern about swap linkages derives from the concentrated interdependence of commitments: "It doesn't have to be the biggest guy on the block that gets into trouble. . . . This is no longer a game of checkers; it's a game of chess."[33]

Note-Issuance Facilities

The profit dynamics on all forms of the note-issuance facility (NIF) instrument matured very quickly as borrowers, without significant credit tiering (which might lead to more organized price tiering),[34] drove arrangement fees down while dropping the interest spread from LIBOR-based to sub-LIBID levels. The underpricing of risk, particularly as the NIFs represented off–balance-sheet commitments by underwriting banks, stimulated regulatory correction. In April 1985 the Bank of England ordered the inclusion of 50 percent of the facility in the calculation of the risk-asset ratio. Shortly thereafter similar moves were taken by the Bank of Japan (30 percent), in January 1986 by the U.S. Federal Reserve (30 percent), and in February 1986 by the Bundesbank (50 percent).

Regulatory action, in and of itself, does not increase returns to banks; the prices borrowers pay do not increase. But at least three subsequent risk-controlling developments can be attributed wholly or in part to the correction. First, the normal facility structure was modified, which permitted the transfer of the underwriting commitment from one bank to another (the transferable underwriting facility, or TRUF). This was of little value from the point of view of systemwide risk but represented an effort by some underwriters to guard against the possibility of regulatory change in their home jurisdictions.

Second, the banks as a group—and particularly those in London—were strongly encouraged to develop a secondary market of investors. In early 1986 it was still possible to remark that "until recently most of the paper was placed with smaller banks . . . placement of paper with non-bank investors is not very highly developed. There are differences of opinion about which banks hold Euronotes. French, Italian, Canadian, Middle Eastern and

[33]MNS interview, 1988.
[34]Gioia M. Parente, *Critical Issues in the Expansion of the Euronote and Eurocommercial Paper Market* (Salomon Brothers, June 1986), p. 6.

(increasingly) Far Eastern (for example South Korean) banks are mentioned as note holders, although no data are available."[35] The subsequent indications that underwriters have been able to deepen and diversify the secondary market are important for the avoidance of concentrated credit risk among a limited number of institutions in the Euromarkets.

Third, commercial banks were pushed to begin controlling the significance of their commitments, which seems to have slowed market expansion somewhat. Some did so by placing limits on the amount of their commitments, with those limits related to a predetermined amount of short-term paper that they would be prepared to fund at short notice. Such an approach has the attraction of explicitly taking into account the bank's overall liquidity management as it might be affected by the contingent commitment. Others opted to limit overall commitments in relation to their capital, including through some percentage formula, the commitment in the bank's gearing ratio. These approaches have become more important as the intentions of borrowers have shifted over time away from arranging the majority of facilities solely as undrawn back-ups.

Improvements in risk control as applied to documentation have also been made. The NIF is not a difficult product to understand. The documentation and legal contract forms on which most NIFs are written are adapted from the standardized documentation already developed for syndicated loans. The move toward master contracts or agreements governing specific contracts and telexed commitments between borrowers and lenders has been fairly swift, and documentation is balanced. Underwriters are protected by covenants developed in syndicated loan contracts, and these typically include either

- Requirements that the borrower that draws down on the facility commit to maintaining a stated ratio of internally generated funds to issued notes or, to the same end, that the borrower use a set percentage of self-generated funds in whatever expenditure NIF proceeds go to; or
- So-called material adverse change clauses, which permit underwriters to withdraw from their legal responsibility to the

---

[35]Bank for International Settlements, *Recent Innovations in International Banking,* p. 27.

Investment Banking Controls

Certain basic tendencies have guided investment bankers in their progressively more sophisticated efforts to understand and manage the risks to which their institutions are exposed. Several generalizations can be made.

A Bias toward Market Risk

These bankers have proceeded from their strengths, which are concentrated in the taking and disposing of positions in tradeable instruments. Years of specialized experience in these areas have prepared investment banks to successfully incorporate and assimilate the market risks attending new instruments ranging from swaps to LDC loans. Despite the accumulation of commercial bank credit officers within their organizations, investment banks are generally less well staffed and prepared for credit risk than are commercial banks. The bias is intrinsic to the business. The banks prosper or not on their ability to turn over their capital, applying and reapplying it to the rising opportunity. The term credit position is not sought out, although as some entrants in the leveraged buyout field have found, it can be difficult to avoid.

Management Information Systems

Improvements in management information systems have been widespread over the past few years and in most cases continue today. One banker highlights the problem for this population: "The MIS is the bank's central nervous system. But investment banks have old systems. These are trade-based systems, and today we need data base systems. [Our bank] has had to build its own software system to build its data base and cross-reference the trade-based system."[44] MIS improvements have primarily introduced or refined credit-exposure limit systems. A second investment bank officer described a three-tier system: (1) the counterparty is evaluated, which produces an internal credit rat-

[44]MNS interview, 1988.

ing that implies a permissable net exposure limit; (2) the bank's exposure recommendation is based on its estimation of market risk for the product; and (3) each counterparty determines an acceptable net exposure by product. The working definition of net exposure for each product (as counted against that limit) is that of worst-case loss, exclusive of margin or collateral put up by the counterparty.

Stronger Credit Teams

Credit strengthening is a long-term development, in some cases going back years but accelerating recently as banks have deepened or added to their normal repertoire credit and as country analysts spend their time partly in marketing and partly in vetting new products and transactions. Apart from the addition of niche specialists such as commercial-bank-trained country-risk analysts, this expansion has been geographical as well. The global firm has credit managers and administrators in New York, London, and Tokyo. At one firm this has produced a credit department staff of forty-seven professionals assigned to the three major centers. At another firm, relatively recent hires have strengthened a system of daily risk-exposure consultation in the three zones. As one respondent put it, "We're always in touch with each other. It's seamless. There's not a chance that anyone anywhere in the firm could slip something in without one of us knowing about it."[45]

Reinforced Rules

Strengthening of house rules on acceptable business has also been apparent. Rules on what is and what is not permissible business have always been present and often have formed an indispensable element of corporate culture, but the collective reawakening of international investment banks to the riskiness of their business has emphasized the importance of explicitly defining and teaching these rules. The rules differ widely by firm. At one they consist predominantly of techniques to cushion the risks of a

[45]MNS interview, 1988.

wide variety of business[46] and at another an explicit unbreachable mandate to do no business with below-investment-grade counterparties.[47]

Product Approvals

Formalizing new product approval and introduction has also changed during the last three years. One banker described the change at his institution, and our survey indicates that his description matches the experience at other top-tier investment banks:

> [Around 1985] the proper way to introduce a new product was to build an alliance. A product originator would find a friend in the back office to guarantee that it could be executed properly [and then push the product forward]. Eventually, however, the credit guys caught on that they were not included in the loop . . . [and] reforms were made. . . . Today, the launching process in the investment banks is more formalized. There is a new-products committee, which includes a representative from credit, from liabilities, from corporate finance, and from capital markets. If run properly, the committee is a very healthy addition. It is actually a clubhouse of co-conspirators that come together to consider a new product. It is not only a control group. There is an advocate of the new product from each of the various sectors of the bank represented on the committee. The trick now is to get enough high-level officials so that the product gets proper attention and enough junior-level officials so that something gets done within a reasonable amount of time. A squad is put together to come back in a week to say whether the product works or not. The product life cycle thereafter is very short.[48]

Applying the Controls

These general changes in commercial-bank risk controls can be applied to techniques and reforms governing business in specific product areas.

[46]MNS interview, 1988.
[47]MNS interview, 1988.
[48]MNS interview, 1988.

Interest-Rate and Currency Swaps

Initially, investment banks entered the swaps market as arrangers. To some degree this has changed. Most institutions now carry a developed portfolio of interest-rate and currency swaps where they are the counterparty or the guarantor (regardless of whether they have actually laid off both sides of the swap).

In seeking to protect themselves from the credit implications of their swap commitments, investment bankers have learned that the credit status of corporate counterparties can change materially with lightning speed. An aspect of credit risk long familiar to their commercial banking counterparts was, in this world, renamed "event risk." In some cases the awakening was a rude one:

> We agreed to an interest-rate swap with [a U.S. company] which was a AA-rated credit at the time. They did an LBO, which happened without warning; it really happened overnight, and they emerged the next day as a CCC- to B-rated company. We looked at that and realized this could happen to any number of businesses we work with. . . . Now we concern ourselves a lot with event risk. You enter a contract with some company and that company could get chased by a raider and do a recapitalization. . . . Now we prepare ourselves against event risk in our documentation so that we have the option to terminate a position or ask for collateral.[49]

Event risk has increased the tendency of investment banks to seek collateral on swap positions as well as to alter their documentation. Credit policy questions now tend to focus on the sorts of businesses and counterparties that can be dealt with without collateral and the kinds of collateral that are acceptable—"for example, if people want to do something new like take second mortgages as collateral on an interest-rate swap."[50] Apart from these changes, however, the interest-rate swap is regarded as a well-understood product where decision efficiency is high.

Currency swaps and a related foreign-exchange business— long-dated forward foreign-exchange contracts—are somewhat

[49]MNS interview, 1988.
[50]MNS interview, 1988.

more troublesome. The difficulty is the term of the agreements: "Even three years ago foreign exchange basically meant six months to one year forward. With currency swaps and long-dated forwards now you can go out ten years in a commitment, and that's a lot of risk."[51] Applicable here are not only the credit considerations of event risk but also the invalidation of the old approaches by currency fluctuation: "Everyone has a problem quantifying the amount of risk in one of these contracts, and for a long time everyone had a pretty standard rule—about 10 percent or so. . . . That's all well and good, but currencies now go up and down so much that it doesn't reflect risk at all. Your risk could be 100 percent."[52]

One consequence for many banks has been a winnowing and curtailing of the list of suitable counterparties for these kinds of products. Another has been the increasingly common practice of writing collateral requirements into contracts with requirements of 5 to 10 percent of the total amount at the outset and stated limits that would trigger a request for more collateral. Nonetheless, the foreign-exchange protection business is one of the hottest, most competitive markets around. Competitive pressures curtail what a bank can get away with in terms of price and collateral protection and push the bank's credit officers to approve business with "the second tier—the lower-investment-grade counterparty."[53] The credit decision has been shaped into a rounder, more integrated judgment of business soundness. There is a clear trend on the part of the credit officer to weigh both appropriate return and the counterparty's overall standing with the bank as elements in what was once a purely up or down credit decision.

Note-Issuance Facilities

The differences between commercial and investment banking practice concerning note-issuance facilities are essentially nonexistent. Few investment banks will even do Euronote business now

[51]MNS interview, 1988.
[52]MNS interview, 1988.
[53]MNS interview, 1988.

unless they are able to combine an arrangement role with an underwriting role, thereby allowing themselves to couple upfront fees with placement earnings when notes are issued.

Leveraged Buyouts

Leveraged buyouts involve risks that may be less familiar to investment bankers than their commercial banking counterparts. Some, but not all, investment banks involved in the business have evolved systematic approaches for the control of these risks. Others curtail their involvement in the market and retain the luxury of considering each go decision at the management committee level. As one investment bank credit officer put it, "We don't do direct loans, . . . only bridge loans. In our case a bridge loan is not a pure credit decision but a business judgment which is done not in the credit department but at a much higher level, like the board level."[54]

This bank's practice leaves us with mixed feelings. In the banking business the credit judgment is neither the sole nor necessarily the most important decision; rounded judgment is called for, particularly as the size and strategic importance of the deal increases. But this bank was risking more than just its partners' capital; it floated a sizeable equity stake on the market prior to our interview, which would seem to call for more rather than less rigorous adherence to credit standards. With a public offering at its back, the firm is called to a high level of fiduciary responsibility.

There are two principal credit risks facing intermediaries: the successful initial placing of bridge loans and the relatively hidden risk of subordinated paper flowing back to the bank. As noted earlier in this chapter, some spectacular failures have occurred when investment bankers moved too quickly into the LBO business. The risks are great precisely because the business involves a calculated, hopefully short-term, breaching of the industry's central rule—the avoidance of concentrated risk.

One LBO manager for an investment bank analyzes the situation neatly:

[54]MNS interview, 1988.

The biggest risks that [our bank] faces today come on the principal side, as when the bank is offering bridge financing by making or guaranteeing a loan. . . . The monitoring of bridge financing has fallen short just as the monitoring of capital markets products did a few years ago. In the first few deals, there were very few people involved. The more people that took part, the more difficult the deal became. Now we have a committee to deal with the relevant questions confronted in bridge financing.[55]

A classic LBO deal has five building blocks: a good company, good management, equity money, senior debt money, and subordinated debt. "The view held by many [early in the market's phase] was that the investment banks could rely on the good housekeeping seal of approval of the commercial bank and therefore not get involved in credit-risk analysis. If the senior loan was in place, so the reasoning went, then the investment bank [providing either equity or subordinated debt money] was not at risk. This turned out not to be true."[56]

A second error was assuming, as some still appear to, that the subordinated debt risk is only short term in nature. Should something go wrong prior to placement, the consequences are stunning: "If you have a huge bridge loan outstanding, you could blow up."[57] It does not follow, however, that once the bank places the converted loan its hands are clean. "This kind of attitude is problematic. Even after the bonds are sold, sooner or later they will end up back with the investment bank, albeit marked to market."[58] Increasing the bank's credit-analysis staff for the long term is proving critical: "We are not good at risk monitoring. Investment banks have to learn to stay in touch and know when there is a problem. But we have developed a 'fire and forget' attitude. We need a long-term monitoring capacity. Investment bankers currently operate like punters, but we have to learn to play on the line."[59]

The practice that is evolving is for investment banks to take equity positions along with their bridge financing. "If the bank is taking the subordinated debt, then it should also have some of

[55]MNS interview, 1988.
[56]MNS interview, 1988.
[57]MNS interview, 1988.
[58]MNS interview, 1988.
[59]MNS interview, 1988.

the equity ownership, for two reasons. This way the bank has a stake in the performance of the company, and further, it can influence the management if there is a problem which is affecting the value of the subordinated debt."[60] Substantial equity positions, either in a few or many companies, however, require a monitoring capacity that is not yet available in top-tier firms.

Not all deals are large, and not all bridge loans measure in the hundreds of millions of dollars. Currently, however, a number of highly leveraged vulnerable bought-out companies must pay down their debt (and at the same time not slash capital spending to the point of crippling the company) before the onset of the next recession. The merchant bankers badly need to develop an analytical capability to avoid serious missteps in a future, possibly more hostile economic environment. Financially, the ultimate risk of the LBO is that asset values will move sharply with the business cycle. The assumed debt burden is not so forgiving.

Systemic Risk: The Cross Committee Report

Whether specific financial market trends raise or lower risk to the system is a difficult question, often discussed but rarely yielding satisfactorily firm conclusions. In the 1970s the discussion centered on the presence of offshore markets, notably the Euromarket, as a destabilizing adjunct to national financial markets. Financial innovation and associated behavior have since raised the question anew and with added urgency.

Most efforts to address the issue of systemic risk are hindered by a lack of definitive evidence. Data either are collected by various national authorities, who are limited both by national boundaries and divergent methods of collection, or do not exist. As a case in point, no one has yet cast suitable methods for measuring broad and narrow measures of money in offshore markets, much less money velocity.

Lack of transparency regarding financial activities outside the domains of supervisory authorities tied to national governments has often placed regulators in the difficult position of trying to infer consequences on the strength of single cases, informal market reports, or second- and third-hand information. This hazard

[60]MNS interview, 1988.

has certainly encouraged the exchange of information between sets of national authorities, and the work of the Study Group established by the Central Banks of the Group of Ten Countries[61] (known as the Cross Committee), took informal exchanges a step forward toward institutionalization. Published in 1986, the committee's report contains the definitive treatment of systemic risk.[62]

The committee examines the claim that the sheer flexibility of new products—their risk-passing and transforming property— lowers net risk at the institutional level by permitting portfolios to be fine-tuned. Over the long term some institutions may fail to correctly judge their ability to manage selected risks, but overall risks to the financial system should be better allocated than before. In terms of a net overall change to the sum of risk itself, the aggregate effect of multiple changes should be merely a summation—no net increase in total risk and an improvement in the quality of risk management.

The committee examined this stance from the contextual viewpoints of total leverage, the market dynamics of underpricing, the dynamics of rapid change in financial markets, the problem of risk concentration, the question of net increased risk arising from options, and finally, the effects of a sustained increase in market volatility.

Total Leverage

For the better part of two decades there has been a visible and general trend in the increase of debt finance and debt stocks in relation to equity and capital reserves. To a great extent this macroeconomic phenomenon is a consequence of the sustained inflation, high in comparison with past levels, to be found throughout the OECD. The commonly appreciated effect is that in periods of inflation the prices of real assets rise to cover the long-term costs of debt. The whole economic structure appears

---

[61]Members included representatives from the central banks of Belgium, Canada, France, Germany, Italy, Japan, Luxembourg, Netherlands, Sweden, Switzerland, United Kingdom, United States, and the Bank for International Settlements, chaired by Mr. Sam Y. Cross of the Federal Reserve Bank of New York.

[62]Bank for International Settlements, *Recent Innovations in International Banking*, pp. 197–220.

capable of supporting a growing load of debt, as more relaxed credit decisions are being made about oil-producing less developed countries, U.S. homeowners, and much of what lies between.

Change sustained for several years—indeed, for a generation in this case—tends to erode equity and capital reserves in relation to assumed debt. Leverage, in a broad and structural sense, increases, eroding the entire structure's capacity to cushion shock or very rapid change. It is not coincidental that quickened innovation and higher leverage in systemic terms should come together. Financial history dating back to the 1700s clearly documents that these phenomena tend to keep company.

Change throughout the economy is not only reflected but may be magnified in the financial sector, which is plastic and responsive and tends to anticipate the trend. The Cross Committee expressed concern that the amount of available equity capital is not adequate in the economy as a whole, and the banking sector in particular. This concern sharpens with the apparent linkage between markets and increased fungibility of money.

The Risk of Underpricing over the Long Term

Anxiety at the broader level shaped the committee's inquiry into the question of whether market dynamics encouraged a behavior of underpricing over the long term. It is not hard to make this argument, in part because recent memory holds so many instances of herd behavior on the part of banking institutions and their widespread tendency to underprice risk: lending to developing countries, oil-sector lending, real estate lending, and in the years to come further confirmation may come in LBOs and even home equity loans. As the committee observed, banking institutions are price takers incapable of dictating to the broader market. In a period of clear overcapacity, this becomes worse. To cite the committee report:

> A given financial institution may well see perfectly clearly, with hindsight, what mistakes were made in lending during the late 1970s, and seek to apply those lessons to the future. In the first

instance, that suggests banks should seek wider profit margins in all activities in order to accumulate greater loss reserves appropriate to the newly perceived risk levels. In fact, banks undertook to widen credit spreads on many categories of loans which involved increased risk, especially after 1982. However, it has proved difficult to maintain wider spreads, partly because of the difficulty borrowers in difficult straits have in paying them and also in the face of competitive pressures.[63]

But the lesson of the experience in the 1970s may lie more in the realisation that longer-term predictive capacities of market participants have not improved. . . . The implication . . . is that, if possible, *all* transactions, and especially innovative ones, should be priced to contain margins for loss above that implied by short-term expectations for overall economic circumstances. *The practical difficulty in applying that approach is, of course, that an institution which does so, contrary to market trends, cannot hope to remain active and competitive in the short term, mainly because the going price in financial markets at any given moment is set by the individual participant willing to accept the thinnest risk spread.* [64]

If markets seriously mistake the pricing of transactions, losses will occur, often after significant delay, which can produce a certain complacency, dilute the capital of the institutions involved, and increase the system's leverage and risk.

The Problem of Rapid Change

Mispricing is compressed and exaggerated in a period of rapid change. First, pricing is predominantly retrospective, regardless of whether prices are arrived at on the strength of the individual's experience or more sophisticated statistical techniques. In a period of rapid change, institutions enter markets more quickly, pursue business more aggressively, tending to both build up sizeable stocks of assets and take on the management of large exposures prior to assimilating the mature experience a full market or business cycle would provide.

[63]It is worth recalling here that the trend in spreads was to narrow. As indicated earlier, for example, between 1985 and 1988 the average spread on loans to LDCs dropped from ninety-two basis points to fifty-seven basis points.
[64]Bank for International Settlements, *Recent Innovations in International Banking*, pp. 203–5, emphasis added.

The newness of a market is roughly proportional to the fragility of its liquidity in times of stress, an informal rule that is justified in part by the practical observation that most innovations occur among a limited number of participants and mature in a relatively brief period of time. To illustrate, we quote from an internal memorandum circulated within one major investment bank following the crash of the perpetual floating-rate note market segment in 1987. The author observes a range of behavior that confirms regulatory fears:

> Two years ago [1985] many houses were looking to develop a presence in the Euromarkets. The FRN market appeared to offer a quick way in. The houses involved hired inexperienced traders and exposed them to the market without guidance from more experienced dealers. These traders experienced only bull markets for a good period of time and, as in all bull markets, bid-offer spreads narrowed. At the same time spreads were narrowing, the size in which traders were prepared to deal was fast increasing (from $1m to $4m in many cases). All of this resulted in the erosion of trading profitability. The requirement to show a return from trading activities resulted in the move towards illegitimate secondary practices such as squeezing, ramping and houses "acting in concert." These practices have brought the market as a whole into ill-repute and have scared investors away.
>
> Many dealers have failed to develop analytical abilities to complement trading abilities. In a market where both credit analysts and product analysts ought to have been in place (to give a proper perception of value), neither have been found. In addition, many houses have not developed the distribution abilities required to place the paper. Lastly, some houses have been overly concerned with league table placings, to the detriment of all else. This has led to the sacrificing of quality for quantity on a vast scale.[65]

Thus rapid change tends to increase risk for two reasons: the assumptions underlying current pricing are borrowed from very recent experience and can prove false, and the associated institutional behavior is heedless and risk-prone.

[65]Internal memorandum to sales force, U.S. investment bank, 1987.

Risk Concentration

Despite the proliferation of new risks, banks still suffer most of their losses in conventional ways. Despite justifiable concern about new risks, it may be the oldest one of all—concentration—that undoes the banks. From a systemic point of view, it is important to know whether financial innovations affect risk concentration.

Recall the data presented earlier regarding the build-up of off–balance-sheet commitments and contingencies on the part of the thinly capitalized money-center banks. This and similar data led Cross Committee members to speculate about hidden concentrations and stimulated the supervisory task of agreeing on an internationally acceptable capital/asset ratio that would bring off–balance-sheet exposures into consideration of capital adequacy and increase transparency at the level of individual institutions.

Accepting the distinction between market risk, "which in the aggregate must sum to zero," and credit risk, "which by its nature cumulates in direct proportion to the volume of financial contracts outstanding,"[66] the committee expressed its concern. The growth in off–balance-sheet assets has been rapid in relation to the stock of assets recorded—somewhat less than fifteen years. Yet the volume of contingent assets booked exceeded the volume of assets recorded on the balance sheet. Clearly the number cannot be taken as a simple value. Many assets are recorded gross but netted or offset in actual practice; others involve nominal sums several times exceeding the actual credit exposure. Nonetheless, fifteen years is a relatively short period of time, and the phenomenon was most advanced among thinly capitalized institutions, the weakest link in the chain. Perhaps most important, the widespread and growing use of negotiable note facilities (off balance sheet) suggested that the forces of innovation were moving toward the creation of either actual or highly probable credit exposures that were neither visible to financial markets as a whole—or counted against the capital of particular institutions.

[66]Bank for International Settlements, *Recent Innovations in International Banking,* p. 203.

Net Increased Price Risk

The committee isolated options as the one innovation that actually concentrated price risk in aggregate terms. Available evidence suggested the market was unbalanced, with few sellers (who accept potentially unlimited risk) but many buyers (whose risk is limited to the loss of commissions on out-of-the-money options)—an evolving structure that "implies that exposure to [price] risk (exchange or interest-rate variations) is transferred from the market generally to a few institutions which manage that risk for a fee."[67]

This trend should balance out in time but in the interim is exacerbated by two closely related phenomenon. The first, elaborated above, relates to pricing errors that tend to occur in new and quickly expanding markets. The second is the equal tendency of risk-prone institutions to absorb high risks. Only a strict minority of risk-prone institutions can be considered aggressive within their risk tolerance—that is, within the capabilities of their managements. Aside from the losses arising in foreign-exchange options in 1984 and 1985, two other notable institutions were to suffer major losses in relatively new options-writing businesses. The Bank of Credit and Commerce International, later to become notorious for widespread laundering of drug money, was one of these and not to be noted for the efficacy of its management. Bankers Trust, which has first-class management, was the other. In this latter instance, the bank allowed a highly successful trader to exploit huge position limits. He, in turn, built such an intricate portfolio of positions that when he resigned to join another firm, the bank found itself incapable of unwinding his positions without accepting significant losses in the process.

Market Volatility

Exchange and interest-rate volatility has increased in recent years as, in most cases, has the short-term volatility of most financial asset prices. This brings with it greater short-term profit oppor-

---

[67]Bank for International Settlements, *Recent Innovations in International Banking,* p. 204.

tunities and implies that the short-term risk of most financial contracts has increased. Without attempting to determine the remote causes of this phenomenon, the Cross Committee observed that a complex relationship exists between volatility and innovation and that many innovations exist to hedge risk arising from volatility. With this, they observe that the high leverage associated with options and futures has become available to a much larger population of speculative investors.

Is wider speculation destabilizing? Economic theory tends to answer this question negatively, arguing that speculators enter markets to arbitrage price differences away and depart markets when arbitrage profits disappear. This is fundamentally stabilizing in a medium- or long-term scenario. The Cross Committee observed that

> if speculation is to work in the stabilizing manner, however, several other conditions need to be met. Speculators need to be a continuous factor in markets; their forecasts must be reasonably correct and reflective of fundamental economic factors; they must refrain from joining "bubbles" or "bandwagons"; and they must not be able to rig the markets in which they participate. These assumptions are largely untrue at certain times, usually for brief intervals, and they are almost never entirely true at any time.[68]

In a justly celebrated passage John Maynard Keynes brilliantly satirized the speculator's eagerness to join in bubbles:

> Most of these persons are, in fact, largely concerned, not with making superior long-term forecasts of the probable yield of an investment over its whole life, but with foreseeing changes in the conventional basis of valuation a short time ahead of the general public. . . . Professional investment may be likened to those newspaper competitions in which the competitors have to pick out the six prettiest faces from a hundred photographs, the prize being awarded to the competitor whose choice most nearly corresponds to the average preferences of the competitors as a whole; so that each competitor has to pick, not those faces which he himself finds prettiest, but those which he thinks likeliest to catch the fancy of the other competitors, all of whom are looking at the problem from

[68]Bank for International Settlements, *Recent Innovations in International Banking,* p. 210.

the same point of view. It is not a case of choosing those which, to the best of one's judgement, are really the prettiest, nor even those which average opinion genuinely thinks the prettiest. We have reached the third degree where we devote our intelligences to anticipating what average opinion expects the average opinion to be.[69]

The problem is not new, and it is deeply rooted in financial markets as such.

The new wrinkle characterizing present markets has been introduced by the new ways in which information is made available and treated by all market participants, individual and institutional. Ten years ago an informal hierarchy of "those in the know" governed most organized markets. At the center were trading institutions that specialized in the interpretation of this information for their clients. That control over information has been lost as an increasingly broad range and number of financially oriented firms have equal access to information and interpretations. Information about financial markets certainly has increased in quantity, but it may have diminished in average quality. In fact, the great increase in purveyors and consumers of information may well have yielded a lower quality of work on both sides of the terminal. The phenomenon would correspond with what we know about rapid change in other markets, prior to their eventual consolidation down to quality producers. In any case, the idea that wider distribution of information has a stabilizing effect on markets rests on the idea that while there will be many interpretations, on average the market will understand the information correctly.

As the Cross Committee noted, there is an alternative hypothesis—namely, that markets can be destabilized if traders react to new information by getting the direction of change in the market right while mistaking the degree or volume of change. Traders may react to new information on the basis of expectations about it and, worse, on the basis of expectations about other partici-

[69]John Maynard Keynes, *The General Theory of Employment, Interest and Money* (New York: Harcourt Brace Jovanovich, 1964), pp. 154–56.

pants' expectations, producing the widely noted overshooting effect seen in financial markets of all kinds.[70]

What emerges, both from the Cross Committee's work and from similar treatments, is a series of arguments and observations that persuasively supports the notion that systemic risk has increased in the period under consideration. Whether innovation itself is the sole culprit or merely one among a host of malefactors beginning with inflation and ending with, perhaps, moral values, is a secondary question, although an important one. Due restraint appears very much to be part of the philosophy of regulatory authorities in effecting the general down-gearing they wish to see among banking institutions.

[70]Bank for International Settlements, *Recent Innovations in International Banking,* p. 211.

3

Commercial Banks: The Organizational Response

Martin Mayer titled the opening chapter of his 1984 work, *The Money Bazaars,* "The Bank Is Dead." Mayer quoted North Carolina National Bank executive Tom Storrs: "A few years ago, you could describe the [U.S.] banking industry as a group of institutions with defined characteristics. In the 1990s, you'll have to describe it as a group of services provided by a range of institutions."[1] That remains a serviceable description of what prevails, even if the financial supermarket concept never fulfilled its promise in the United States. (For good reason, most people still fail to make the connection between Sears and banking.) Considerable strategic change has occurred in all aspects of banking, not least in the portion of the international sphere examined in this chapter.

Changing Bank Strategies

For most large international commercial banks, the period from 1982 to 1984 was a time for self-examination as returns diminished, asset quality declined, and market structures began to crumble. The years 1985 to 1987 represent a period of strategic

[1]Martin Mayer, *The Money Bazaars: Understanding the Banking Revolution around Us* (New York: New American Library, 1985), p. 1.

recommitment or withdrawal as managements cast their lots with or against the international market.

In 1985 four basic strategies were available for international commercial banks: (1) continue with conventional commercial banking, effected in several markets; (2) restructure in favor of fee-generating products and merchant-banking commitments and slim existing balance-sheet assets in the process; (3) for the indecisive, follow a compromise strategy—politely termed *hybrid*—that mixed some combination of the first two strategies with the hopeful language of strategy papers about market selection and cherry picking; or (4) retreat from international lending and international commitments altogether.[2]

U.S. regional banks, including the superregionals, nearly universally opted for the fourth strategy. In important respects, this decision was sensible and represented their natural propensity. Few had far-flung international networks or substantial commitments, and nearly all were actively engaged in international finance only in the areas of short-term trade finance and correspondent banking. In practical terms, their retreat from international banking meant active slimming of LDC loans (most of which were acquired as subparticipations from larger banks in New York or Chicago) and returning to the basic businesses and markets that they knew well. The query "What are we paying those people in London for anyway?" was not so difficult to answer—a "no-brainer," in the words of one regional banker.[3]

Large multinational money centers—U.S., Canadian, and British—occupied a different market and were faced with much more difficult choices. Leaving aside the option of muddling through (the third strategy above), their choices basically came down to doing what they had always done or doing something new.

The Status Quo

From 1978 to 1986 several forces dovetailed to reduce the allure of conventional commercial banking. One was the disastrous

---

[2]A comprehensive look at the international businesses of regional banks during this period can be found in Multinational Strategies, *Regional Banks: International Strategies for the Future* (New York: MNS, 1987).
[3]MNS interview, 1986.

performance of some of the largest commercial-banking custom-ers, particularly sovereign customers, in Latin America, Southeast Asia, and Africa.[4] Another was the heightened scrutiny of bank regulators. A vigorous campaign to strengthen bank capital and management controls to slow the deterioration of asset quality meant that adding new assets to the balance sheet became a more costly proposition.

Capital Costs

At year end 1982 large U.S. banks were sitting on average capital-adequacy ratios of 4.8 percent. Peer institutions in the United Kingdom and Canada were in a similar condition. Smaller banks fared better, with an average ratio of 5.5 percent. By the end of 1986 the ratio for large banks had grown to 7.1 percent, a rise of 48 percent. Small banks increased their capital-adequacy ratio by almost 30 percent to 7.0 percent.[5]

Higher capital-adequacy rules meant that, for a large bank, the capital cost of each additional booked loan was 48 percent higher. Not surprisingly, this affected portfolio growth. In 1981 and 1982 average loans and leases extended by these banks increased by 12.7 percent and 13.3 percent, respectively. In 1983, with the onset of the debt crisis, average loans and leases increased by only 6.3 percent. The pace picked up again in 1984, when the growth rate was 12.7 percent, but declined steadily thereafter (7.4 percent in 1985 and 5.6 percent in 1986).[6]

In banks where blemished portfolios constrained asset growth, there were clear implications for the analysts—whether econo-mists, country-risk analysts, or pure credit managers—charged with the task of analyzing international risks. Many reported to us that a considerable amount of their time was directed toward

[4]As of December 1982 exposure to Brazil represented over 49 percent of the capital of the nine largest U.S. banks. Mexico accounted for over 45 percent. Total exposure in Latin America alone represented approximately 159 percent of capital. These figures are adapted from Multinational Strategies, *Regional Banks: International Strategies for the Future*, p. 44.
[5]These figures are adapted from Thomas Hanley, James Rosenberg, Carla D'Arista, Neil Mitchell, and Jay Rodin, *A Review of Bank Performance* (New York: Salomon Brothers, 1987), p. 54.
[6]These figures were adapted from Thomas Hanley, James Rosenberg, Carla D'Arista, Neil Mitchell, and Jay Rodin, *A Review of Bank Performance* (Salomon Brothers, April 1985), p. 33, and (April 1987), p. 39.

managing relationships with regulators. More work was distributed on fewer desks, since declining profits spurred staff cutbacks in cost centers.

Size and Efficiency: Another Growth Constraint

Bankers were also grappling in practical terms with an old but still muddled question regarding size and efficiency. Since the early 1980s there has been a heated debate over the existence of economies of scale in the U.S. banking system. Bankers, regulators, and academics examined average costs in banking to determine whether these costs fall as a bank grows in size, thereby increasing profitability, and if so, whether there is a point after which average costs stop falling—or perhaps rise again.

The existing evidence on economies of scale in banking is inconclusive. Two studies identify maximum efficiencies at banks with deposits of $100 million or less.[7] But a study out of the Federal Reserve Bank of New York comments—with dry understatement—that "the sustained financial viability of banking institutions 1000 times the size of the (supposedly) largest efficient banks strongly suggests that the diseconomies which some have observed at smaller levels are local rather than global."[8] This study found that optimal economies of scale were achieved by banks with assets of between $15 billion and $37 billion.

Coming at it from a different angle, Jon Moynihan of First Manhattan Consulting Group took a look at large bank takeovers. Of the twenty-six large banks that made purchases in 1982 greater than 10 percent of their size, only six (23 percent) performed better than similar banks that did not expand. The shares of banks that made similar purchases in 1983 performed 20 percent worse in the following year than those of banks that refrained from making acquisitions. Banks that made purchases in

[7]George Bentson, Gerald Hanweck, and David Humphrey, "Scale Economies in Banking: A Restructuring and Reassessment," *Journal of Money, Credit, and Banking* 14 (1982): 435–56, and Thomas Gilligan, Michael Smirlock, and William Marshall, "Scale and Scope Economies in the Multi-Product Banking Firm," *Journal of Monetary Economics* 13 (1984): 393–405.
[8]Sherrill Shaffer and David Edmond, "Economies of Superscale and Interstate Expansion," *Federal Reserve Bank of New York*, No. 8612 (Nov. 1986): 1.

1984 were still 12 percent behind their peers three years later, in terms of share prices.[9]

Importance of Cutting Costs. Researcher David Humphrey has made an illuminating point. Based on data taken in the late 1970s and early 1980s, he admits that economies of scale probably exist and that identifying them could shed light on important matters of public policy. He goes on to point out, however, that on close inspection, economies of scale may not be the heart of the matter. He found that banks of roughly the same size have widely dispersed average costs and that this dispersion is greater than the differences in average costs between banks of different sizes. It is common for a large and a small bank to have similar costs while two banks identical in size have very different costs. If the objective is to cut costs, then growing to an optimal size is probably much less important to the bank than cutting costs in other ways that have nothing to do with economies of scale.[10] This conclusion is useful and matches the practical experience of bankers. It suggests that commercial banking has been, until recently, an industry forgiving of inefficiencies. Banks with high cost structures compared to their peers have nevertheless been able to survive and flourish. This makes intuitive sense. As a highly regulated industry (although less highly regulated now), banks were barred from certain profitable activities but also were protected from competition in markets regarded as their proper domain.

With the partial dismantling of barriers to competition, traditional commercial-banking markets lost some of their dynamism. Under attack from new competitors, banks have reoriented their attention to cutting costs wherever possible and generating earnings without adding new assets. Conventional commercial banking, at least those parts of it that have enjoyed the luxury of being relatively inefficient, is no longer coveted business.

As a result, the pace of asset build-up among U.S. banks slackened. Within the United States, bank rankings have undergone

[9]As quoted in "Survey: International Banking," *Economist,* March 26, 1988, p.16.
[10]David Humphrey, "Cost Dispersion and the Measurement of Economies in Banking," *Economic Review* 73 (3) (May/June 1987): 24–38.

important changes as the link between size and growth has loosened. Money-center banks grew at an average rate of 7.9 percent from 1980 to 1986, whereas regional banks grew by 10.3 percent annually for the same period.[11] Internationally, the same phenomenon was seen as U.S. and British banks tended to slide down the conventional rankings of bank by size, yielding place more often than not to institutions on the continent and in Japan.

The main force behind the growth of Japanese banks was the precipitous fall in the value of the dollar. In 1982 one dollar bought about 250 yen, but by 1988 it could buy only half as many. Among the many consequences of the strong yen for the international financial community was to bloat Japanese banks compared to their U.S. counterparts. If all banks had been frozen in 1982, Japanese banks would have watched their yen-denominated assets, deposits, and capital base virtually double in terms of dollars. The effects of this are difficult to measure with any precision, but it certainly sparked a psychological change in the U.S. banking community that increased the competitive heat it was already experiencing. The quest for efficiency took on new urgency.

The sheer size of Japanese banks also raised the specter of large Japanese investments in the U.S. banking industry. U.S. banks were no longer too large to be swallowed. The fall of the dollar reduced share prices by one-half in yen terms. If they wanted to avoid being a target by an outside investor, U.S. banks had to strengthen their share prices in other ways to counter the effect of exchange-rate changes. This was a tall order in the convulsive years of the early 1980s. The negative consequences of inefficiency were coming home to roost just as the dollar began to tumble, compounding the challenge facing U.S. commercial banks. Share prices reflected this to some extent. In 1980 the shares of the ten largest U.S. banks were trading at 76.0 percent of their book value, on average.[12] By 1982 the average fell to 68.4

---

[11]Figures are extrapolated from assets totals provided in Hanley, Rosenberg, D'Arista, Mitchell, and Rodin, *A Review of Bank Performance* (April 1985), p. 35, and (April 1987), p. 39.

[12]Share prices and bank sizes are based on information from Hanley, Rosenberg, D'Arista, Mitchell, and Rodin, *A Review of Bank Performance* (1985, 1987). Share prices are for Decem-

percent, mainly due to the shock waves of Mexico's threat to halt debt-service payments in August of that year.

The subsequent effort to improve bank health focused on stricter capital-adequacy requirements and partially reversed this downward trend. In 1986 shares of the ten banks were trading at 90.4 percent of their book value, far better than they had at any other time during the decade. But the recovery hides some interesting disparities. If two banks are removed from the measure—J. P. Morgan & Co. and Bankers Trust—the average market-to-book ratio falls to 79.6 percent. In other words, except for these two institutions, most banks did little better than recover the strength they had lost between 1980 and 1982. The threat of foreign bidders eager to exploit the fall of the dollar has not been countered with stronger share prices.

It is no coincidence that Bankers Trust and J. P. Morgan & Co., the two banks that have performed the best, also relied the least on traditional commercial banking, although in slightly different ways. J. P. Morgan & Co. traditionally has been a conservative institution that resisted expansion at the cost of profits. Its capital-adequacy ratios have consistently exceeded the industry standard (only in 1984 did it not set the upper limit). A long-established concentration on wholesale banking could be transformed with relative ease into more of a merchant-banking approach, an advantage enjoyed by no other U.S. institution. Bankers Trust distinguishes itself by having taken a dramatic leap away from commercial banking and into merchant banking.

Organizational Tensions

An important consequence of changes in commercial banking in the 1980s is the emergence of powerful constituencies within the banks advocating a retreat from commercial banking. As other lines of business became more important, bankers associated with

---

ber 31 of each year. Bank size was determined on the basis of average total assets. The ten banks are Citicorp, Bank of America, Chase Manhattan Bank, Manufacturers Hanover Trust, J. P. Morgan & Co., Chemical Bank, First Interstate Bank, Bankers Trust, Security Pacific Bank, and First Chicago.

them gained in stature. In particular, those who were in merchant-banking areas—involved in such activities as mergers and acquisitions, asset sales, and various forms of underwriting—were looked on as the vanguard of commercial banking's new age. This kind of adulation brought them political influence within their banks as well.

As the rising merchant-banking class battled with the defenders of old-style commercial banking, it was more than a disagreement over policy; it was a cultural clash. The rift was over the style of banking and not just the substance. Merchant bankers prided themselves on being deal-oriented, trained to race against the clock in order to put the deal to bed and then move on to the next client. The name of the game was to minimize the bank's exposure to the client. The old guard championed relationship banking. Long-term ties with customers were assiduously cultivated—and maintained with long-term exposures.

Different standards accompanied different styles. Fee-based income associated with merchant banking has tended to be more lucrative (compared to the amount of capital utilized in the transaction). But it also tends to be much more volatile. By contrast, the very essence of commercial banking is to lock in a decent return over a long period of time. Yet the merchant bankers could not help applying their standards to other areas of the bank. The common argument was that capital should be allocated by rate of return, a bank divided by business line, each measured for annual profitability, and devil take the hindmost.

These were the pressures—fierce competition from other banks and political clashes within—that commercial banks adapted to in the 1980s. Change had to occur. The largest commercial banks diversified into merchant banking. Not only did they enter new lines of business, but they grafted onto their organizations new ways of operating, often modeled after investment banks. Some major banks have gone much further down this road than others, but few, if any, have escaped the trend.

Organizational politics, in some cases, produced backlashes as cultures stubbornly refused to meld, yielding in turn an organizational line of political compromise and hybrid strategies. Chase Manhattan was one example. In 1987 and 1988 the top office holders in the investment banking operations were replaced with officers with corporate lending backgrounds. Subsequent reports of recriminations and charges that commercial bankers were settling old scores painted a troubled picture.

One such was Richard P. Urfer, previously chief operating officer of Chase Manhattan Capital Markets. In the wake of the reorganization he observed, "The basic problem is that investment banking and commercial banking are very different. The basic difference is that the investment banker should be representing the owner. If you're a lender, you've got to be representing your own capital and the corporation. The philosophies are very different. Many of the problems stem from that."[13]

Merchant Banking

Merchant banking is a term that describes the recent bank strategies of actively buying and selling loans instead of simply creating them and holding them to term, and of offering services—capital-markets products, to use the dominant parlance—other than typical loans. Commercial banks are pitted most squarely against investment banks when they offer interest-rate and currency swaps, note-issuance facilities, and a variety of other products that restructure a borrower's obligations and generate liquidity. In this book the term *merchant banking* encompasses both strict merchant-banking and capital-market activities.

Commercial banks in the United States and elsewhere have been pursuing limited variations on the merchant-banking theme since the early 1980s, when banks began to experiment with transactions in the Euromarkets that were prohibited in their home jurisdictions. Subsequent changes in domestic regulation opened new vistas for banks interested in merchant banking, but the wholesale move into merchant banking did not occur until 1985 and 1986.

[13]Robert Guenther, "Investment Bankers Lose Out in Chase Reorganization," *Wall Street Journal,* May 4, 1988, p. 26.

The Stakes in Play

In theory, merchant banking is no different from classic commercial banking. Merchant banking begins with the creation of an asset—that is, a loan. The credit analysis, pricing analysis, and logistical aspects of loan creation are the same for commercial and merchant banking. In classic commercial banking, however, asset creation is referred to as *lending.* Merchant bankers have another term for it—*origination.* Although the difference is purely semantic, it implies an important distinction: *lending* suggests that the bank will hold the loan to term, while *origination* suggests that it will be actively sold.

Even the sale of assets, a key component of the merchant-banking strategy, is not new to commercial banking. In fact, the huge growth in lending to Third World countries was aided by loan syndication, a variant on loan sales in which a lead bank negotiates and prepares the terms of a large loan and then sells participation in it to several other banks. Since the onset of the debt crisis in 1982 banks have sold debt on the secondary market and swapped it among themselves, two other variants on asset sales.

The shift from commercial to merchant banking has not required a drastic reeducation. The main change has been in management perspective rather than in the mechanics of banking. Institutions pursuing the merchant-banking strategy have changed the way they make operational decisions, even though these decisions are carried out using mechanisms familiar to most international commercial bankers. Yet decision-making modes are the variables that define the way an institution is to be organized. For this reason the merchant-banking strategy has caused considerable reorganization in the major commercial banks.

Shift to Portfolio Management

One important change is that a bank's basket of assets is managed as a unified portfolio rather than a conglomerate of parallel but independent assets. The portfolio approach to management has elevated the status of asset sales to that of loan origination. Under the classic commercial banking mode, the sale of an asset was considered a second-best option to be used only when the optimal option—holding the loan to term—met with a problem. In merchant banking a loan is originated either because the bank wants to hold on to it or because it wants to sell it off; both options are compared in terms of their relative costs and benefits. There is no presumption that the loan will be held to maturity.

Failing this presumption, what standards guide the decision? Herein lies the distinguishing feature of the portfolio management approach. The decision is based on the bank's goal to maintain a specifically defined mix of assets in its portfolio. Originations and sales are conducted with this goal in mind. Moreover, merchant banking implies the active purchasing of loans from other banks or investors in order to achieve the proper mix. Of course, this is not the sole criterion. Loans are also originated, bought, and sold because a bank believes that it might reap the differential between price of undervalued asset and its long-term price, the same way securities are traded. Finally, a bank can earn healthy fees for originating a loan even if it does not want to retain the loan in its portfolio.

Perhaps the overriding force pushing banks toward the portfolio approach was the need to reduce risk. As a senior credit officer at a large U.S. bank put it, "If you felt that you could only take loans that were coming down the pike and you had to hold them, there is a lot less incentive to do the kind of work that we are trying to do. If you feel you have some flexibility in what you buy and what you sell, and your origination does not have to be tied with what you retain, then there is more incentive to use the portfolio approach. We have always been good at originating, and our appetite before was to keep the risk. We are now not in a position to do that any more."[14]

Reorganization by Product Line

Another change in management perspective is the organization of activities by bank product rather than by borrower. This change

[14]MNS interview, 1988.

has been driven not only by the shift from commercial to strict merchant banking but by the emergence of other capital-market products offered by commercial banks. Historically, commercial banks offered customers a limited variety of services primarily centered around the conventional medium-term loan. It made little sense to organize the institution around different services. Instead, banks arranged their international departments based on the characteristics of borrowers. Customers from a certain geographic region were grouped under a single chain of command for that region. Sometimes departments were created based on specific industries.

Increasingly, however, banks are reorganizing their departments by product. For example, banks have established separate departments under headings such as *corporate lending* and *capital markets.* A single customer might approach a bank for both a five-year loan and an interest-rate swap. A relationship would be developed between the customer and each of the departments.

Implications for Risk Analysis

Part of the rationale for such reorganizations is the evolving demand for international risk analysis and management. The presumption beneath the organization of classic commercial banking is that the single most important component of risk is credit risk. In other words, an assessment of a five-year loan to an international customer requires first and foremost an evaluation of the creditworthiness of the particular borrower. Exogenous factors such as interest-rate and currency shifts are important but secondary.

New products have taken risk assessment beyond traditional bounds, elevating other sources of risk to a par with credit risk. This is not to say that new products are riskier than the classic bank loan, but they do combine the various sources of risk differently and therefore complicate decisions. Banks have found that the process is simplified if separate risk-assessment approaches are developed for each product, since the methodology often varies considerably from product to product, so risk is increasingly being managed by product rather than by borrower.

The reorganization of the institution by product is partly an elaboration of this.

Portfolio thinking and organization by product have placed a new set of demands on commercial banks. All banks report that the pace of activity has quickened, particularly in some of the capital-market products. Complicated risk analysis and management also requires bank officers to marshall expertise and resources from several different areas in addition to credit analysts, including market analysts, lawyers, accountants, and others. In order to meet these demands fluidly, some banks have radically reformulated their organizational charts.

The Case of Bankers Trust

Bankers Trust has made a concerted move toward merchant banking. While other banks were tiptoeing into merchant banking—creating discrete business units while leaving the mainstream commercial bank intact—Bankers Trust thoroughly revamped its basis structure. The bank has set the outer bound for other commercial banks moving into merchant banking.

Exit from Retail Banking

One of the first steps in the process was the divestiture of the bank's retail operations and a consequent downsizing. Then the bank commenced a wholesale internal reorganization and restructuring of the transaction processes. Every new loan decision now involved four parties: (1) marketing (the lenders or loan originators), (2) funding (those in charge of raising funds for the loan), (3) syndicating (those responsible for the potential sale of the loan), and (4) credit (those asked to assess the credit quality and figure in a risk-pricing component).

The person associated with this transformation is Charles Sanford, now chairman of the bank. Throughout the reorganization Sanford made his objectives clear. The new goal of Bankers Trust was the "creation of a hybrid institution that combines commercial with investment banking, and does away entirely with consumer services. A key part of this strategy is to convert all of the bank's corporate loans into the equivalent of interest bearing bonds that can be sold to investors."[15] The first steps were to sell the retail banking and credit-card operations and to stop making unprofitable loans to large corporate customers.

Active Asset Management

The next step was to actively sell loans. Loan selling would provide the bank with "an immediate replacement of the cash that has been lent, rather than having to wait years until the loan is repaid. And selling the loan means that Bankers Trust does not have to keep capital on hand to back them. That is a relief at a time when Federal regulators are raising capital requirements for banks because of the rash of loan defaults in recent years." In 1984 the bank sold $7.2 billion of loans to corporate customers, representing 30 percent of its total loan portfolio. The aim was to "securitize" the portfolio. According to Mr. Sanford, "I think you can liquidize 90 percent of the loan portfolio. There is very little you can't sell at a price."[16]

Increased Trading

Trading operations also have grown in the past few years, especially in foreign exchange. These markets have been anything but stable, yet Bankers Trust has managed to earn huge profits. In 1987 Bankers reaped an income of $593 million from foreign-exchange transactions, 1.02 percent of its average total assets. The closest contenders earned less than one-third as much as a proportion of average total assets.[17] It has been a bold performance, especially for a commercial bank. Indeed, observers frequently admit to an uneasiness toward Bankers. Ira Stepanian, chief executive officer of the Bank of Boston, reminds us that "any company that makes a lot of money from trading can also lose that

[15]Robert A. Bennett, "Sanford's New Banking Vision," *New York Times,* March 17, 1985, Section 3, p. 1.
[16]Ibid.
[17]Guenther, "Investment Bankers Lose Out in Chase Reorganization."

much."[18] But Bankers Trust is undaunted by the riskier side of the merchant-banking strategy.

Internal Change

A consequence of this was a wholesale organizational restructuring. The bank reorganized around new functional units as well as new territorial or geographic lines. The new functional units are groups such as Global Processing, Trading, and Marketing. In addition, the bank's international operations were dispersed among geographic units—Europe/Middle East/Africa, North America, and Latin America/Pacific—each run by an executive vice president. The geographic reorganization, however, is intended to be an intermediary step until these units are replaced by purely functional units.

The lending business (and several other lines) is conducted by the geographic units. If, for instance, the Latin America/Pacific unit wants to purchase a new bank, that unit, rather than a separate acquisition unit, would purchase the bank. Global Processing, by contrast, handles all money transfer business as well as letters of credit.

The process of transformation was not easy. The bank's culture was traditionally directed toward lending and marketing, and lending officers had an incentive to create "bonusable" events like developing a new relationship or closing a creative deal. Now lending officers are acutely aware of the risk dimensions of their work. Each officer or group is assigned a capital charge for loans whereby the return on the loans must compensate for the risk they involve. The concept of a capital charge is to restructure incentives by placing all deals on a level playing field and adjusting the hurdle according to the asset's quality. Lending officers can make loans as they determine, but each event is handicapped accordingly by the capital charge. There has been some resistance to this approach from within the bank.

[18]As quoted by Sarah Bartlett, "Bankers Trust Could Beat the Street at Its Own Game," *Business Week*, April 4, 1988, 87.

The final goal has been to implement a system that rates every customer and every deal. The system allows for a relationship to be rated differently from a deal: a decision to hold a loan, sell it, or sell part of it is made on deal-specific terms (the deal's financial soundness) and global terms (how well it fits into the bank's portfolio).

A palpable result of Bankers Trust's shift to merchant banking was the rise in salaries. To hire new staff from Wall Street broker-age houses and securities firms, Bankers had to match the high salaries that were the norm on Wall Street. The average salary of the bank's employees increased from $19,105 in 1979 to $33,085 in 1983 and $41,760 in 1984. Bonuses often amounted to one-and-a-half times annual salary.[19]

Pitfalls of the New Strategy

Bankers Trust has transformed itself in the last several years, but most large U.S. banks have moved in a similar direction. This movement has not been achieved without criticism. One view is that there is a psychological limit to the conversion of loans into tradeable commodities—that customers will tolerate only so much of the selling and passing along of their loans. Pushing the merchant-banking concept too far risks jeopardizing the underlying relationship and the bank's due diligence operations. Eager to sell a loan to investors once it has been originated, a bank might gloss over worrisome aspects of the borrower that would be taken more seriously if the loan were to be held to term.

Criticism of this nature takes on added weight as the returns in merchant-banking and capital-market activities have diminished. New products, such as swaps, go through a product cycle as do other goods, and by the end of the cycle they are far less attractive than they were at the beginning. A senior officer at a money-center bank told us that, for example, "Interest-rate swaps went through a very rapid product cycle, as did MOFs and other liquidity guarantee products. They enjoyed a short half-life

[19]Bennett, "Sanford's New Banking Vision."

during which the bank enjoyed supranormal profits. It did not take long for them to be traded like commodities."[20]

Under this kind of dynamic the tendency is at first to move too far in one direction and only later to retreat to a more modest position. Returns at the beginning of the product cycle are lucrative and easy to estimate but fall over the product cycle as more firms offer similar services. Because the long-term returns are difficult to estimate, strategic planning tends to attach inordinate weight to short-term returns. Skeptics fear that this kind of decision making can take a bank into dangerous waters beyond the point at which returns compensate for risks.

Detractors also wonder about other merchant-banking services that could jeopardize good customer relationships. Merger and acquisition activities draw the most fire. Citibank ran afoul of the Dee Corporation in early 1988 when the bank provided money to Barker and Dobson in a hostile takeover bid. Dee opted to cut its relations with Citibank in protest, a move that destroyed a deep relationship: Citibank was agent for Dee's commercial paper and convertible bond issues and depository bank for its American Depository Receipt program; Citibank also extended borrowing facilities to a large Dee subsidiary.[21]

J. P. Morgan & Co. suffered two blows in early 1988. In January Morgan agreed to represent Hoffman–La Roche in its hostile bid for Sterling Drug, a long-time Morgan client. When Hoffman lost the bid to Eastman Kodak, many questioned whether Morgan— the conservative commercial bank—should have jeopardized its Sterling relationship.[22] Later, Morgan angered Corning Glass Works, whose chair was a Morgan director, by advising Smith-Kline Beckman in its takeover attempt of International Clinical Laboratories. SmithKline and Corning were competing with each other in the bid. Corning's chair seriously considered resigning from the Morgan board, according to press reports.[23]

[20]MNS interview, 1988.
[21]Martin Dickson, "When Relations Are Put to the Test," *Financial Times,* Jan. 7, 1988, p. 19.
[22]Leslie Wayne, "How the Morgan Bank Struck Out," *New York Times,* Feb. 7, 1988, section 3, p. 1.
[23]Robert Guenther, "Morgan's Adviser Role in Takeover Fight Strains Relationship with an Old Client," *Wall Street Journal,* April 13, 1988, p. 6.

Changes in the Analysis and Management of Risk

Dramatic changes in commercial-bank strategies require a new way of assessing and controlling risk. New lines of business have brought commercial banks a new array of risks, and most conventional bankers have not had the technical know-how—at least not in the right measure—to cope with their new exposure to currency fluctuations, interest-rate changes, and similar dynamics. Over the past several years commercial banks have been busily acquiring this technical knowledge and adapting their organizations to it. Thus organizational change reflects the demands of risk assessment in a new environment and the fact that commercial banks cannot overhaul their organizations entirely. Certain rigidities and biases are hard to overcome.

Dealing with the Debt Crisis

Indeed, commercial banks did not adapt in earnest until the onset of the debt crisis. Although many of the changes in bank strategy have little to do with Third World debt, the crisis nonetheless catalyzed bank regulators and officers to reevaluate existing systems for assessing and managing risk. The first reaction by banks was to limit damage and quickly halt any activities that might lead the institution into more serious trouble. Some banks set up elaborate systems to achieve these goals. At one New York bank loan officers were made responsible for bad loans. Instead of assigning loans to a work-out unit, the bank made the officer responsible for working out the loan, creating a double disincentive to make an unwise loan: the bad loan stayed with an officer as that officer moved from one assignment to another, and the obligation to work out a problem loan diverted energy away from new lending activities. Several officers in the Latin America division of another bank reportedly did not receive their annual bonuses because they booked what turned out to be bad loans. More dramatic were the negligence suits filed by Bank of America and Chase Manhattan Bank against senior officers because of their decisions.

These changes in strategy yielded modest benefits, but they did not address the central changes taking place in international commercial banking. A more systematic vetting of transactions needed to be constructed to cope with not only existing assets gone sour but also new transactions whose risks were unknown. Most of the banks we reviewed built more checks and balances into the country-limits-setting process to offset a bias toward unrestrained lending characteristic of the 1970s. New international exposures, especially those involving new financial products, were not cut back, but the mechanisms for constraining loans were improved.

One of the top New York banks offers a good example. Up to and through the immediate aftermath of the debt crisis, this bank maintained a classic "czar" system for setting country limits under which the bank's chair made most important international credit decisions individually. This began to change with the retirement of that man. According to a senior bank officer, "Afterwards, when we. had three vice chairmen and were in the Latin American situation, all limits past $2.5 billion were reviewed at top management level."[24]

Shortly thereafter the bank formalized this process by creating a country-risk committee comprised of most of the bank's top executives. This committee, which met about once a month, looked at large exposures and discussed issues such as how to book interest-rate swaps. This system was inadequate, however, by a bank officer's own admission: "It's hard to get them together for more than thirty minutes a month. You would put Brazil to them, but with it all condensed down so they can make their decision in three to four minutes. You go in and you might say, 'I've been agonizing over this for four days now, this is what I've come up with, will you bless it?' And usually they do. Once every two years or so they reverse you."[25]

Banks went further. About half of the banks covered in this study formed separate work-out units to handle sovereign-debt problems. For example, a major midwestern bank organized a special work-out committee in the aftermath of the Mexico debt

[24]MNS interview, 1985.
[25]MNS interview, 1985.

crisis and later expanded the unit to cover commercial as well as sovereign credit. The unit was located in the international banking group, although line officers were not involved in its operation. Similarly, a New York money-center bank created a special work-out group under a bank vice president.

Rapid changes in response to the debt crisis tested the resilience of many banks by taking up time and scarce manpower. In some cases the responsibilities of the country-risk-analysis units were diverted from loan-related analyses toward evaluations of debtor-country economic policies. Banks with large international units were able to assign senior officers and staff to new committees to negotiate agreements with debtor countries, but many banks with smaller international units were unable to spare bank officers for committee responsibilities. In short, banks not only had to respond to a new demand for risk management because of the debt crisis, they also had to make changes in order to relieve the stress created in the process.

At the same time, a conceptual change was taking place in the way banks managed international risk. The country-limits system, whereby officers set a ceiling on the total exposure a bank tolerated in a particular country, began losing its appeal. The coincidence of the debt crisis on one hand and new merchant-banking activities on the other caused country differences to become more pronounced. For problem debtors the notion of a country limit was academic; banks were not increasing their exposures except as part of mandated restructuring agreements. By definition the country limit was equal to the bank's current exposure.

One consequence of this approach to the debt crisis was that banks did less of their own international risk analysis. At the same time, however, banks were eager to move into new markets in the creditworthy countries and therefore did not want to restrain the enthusiasm of their transactors. An officer at one bank told us that his bank's concept of a country limit was particularly soft, allowing the virtually unrestrained growth of country exposures in "quality" nations: "There are about twenty European countries where, because the market for their paper is so good that the paper can be readily sold, we count as little as 25 percent of the full value of the asset toward the limit and can regard the maturity as under one year (even if it isn't)."[26]

Redefining Internal Controls

Genuine change in risk analysis and management began with the search for ways to correct the imbalance between banks' new basket of transactions and their old limits system. All commercial banks have revised their conceptual approach to risk analysis by integrating more factors into any risk analysis, including the effects of changing interest rates, exchange rates, and volatility in the secondary market for assets that commercial banks are creating and holding. Decision structures have evolved to complement these conceptual changes, and more disciplines are brought into risk decisions, including lawyers, accountants, and marketers. An officer from a large midwestern bank described his system:

> We have a new product review cycle through which all new products pass. Every new product has to hit the audit people, the country-risk people, the lawyers, et cetera. That process wasn't in place when some of the exotica were created. The exotica led to the implementation of this process a year and a half ago [the end of 1986]. Senior credit people may decide to use a truncated process to combine due diligence with speed and recognize that you need to get to the market quickly with these things because the life cycle is so short.[27]

Risk analysis also has become more product specific. Bank officers frequently mention that the standard risk assessment that served many purposes in the past is no longer adequate. Analyses must be tailored to the specifications of each transaction, such as its term, interest rate, and currency denominations. This challenged many an analyst who thought only in terms of a single bank product. A senior analyst at a money-center bank commented that "the bank might set a relatively high limit for domestic currency exposure while shying away from hard currency

[26]MNS interview, 1985.
[27]MNS interview, 1988.

exposure. Country risk must deal with this decomposition of risk by type of transaction."[28]

Internal Tensions

The integration of different disciplines into risk analysis has not always proceeded smoothly. Some banks conceive of everything in terms of credit risk—that is, the risk posed by a particular counterparty—and view the effects of exchange rates, interest rates, and market swings simply as an embellished portrayal of the credit risk that can be subsumed into a measure of credit risk. For others, credit risk is conceptually distinct from other kinds of risk (market risk, in short) and one cannot be subsumed by the other.

For many transactions, the point is moot. A five-year loan from a U.S. bank to a U.S. corporation contains market risk in theory. If the bank decides to sell the loan, it exposes itself to the price fluctuations of that kind of loan in the secondary market. But such considerations are rarely as important as the ability of the corporation to meet its obligations—that is, credit risk. Hence, a simple limits system that puts a cap on bank exposure to a specific obligor is enough to manage exposure.

On the other hand, a thirty-year bond issued by the U.S. government bears some credit risk: there is a chance, however slim, that the government will not be able to meet its obligations to the bond holder. Market risk, however, is most important. In this case, banks—and any firm actively trading government bonds and similar securities—establishes limits on the size of open positions that the institution will hold. These limits are based on the volatility of the price of that security rather than on the intrinsic characteristics of the obligor.

Yet many new bank transactions have incorporated roughly equal elements of credit and market risk. For transactions on the cusp between market and credit risk, bank managers must decide which category of risk will dominate. Not surprisingly, those advocating credit supremacy have prevailed over advocates of a

[28]MNS interview, 1988.

market-risk approach. The credit approach squares with commercial banking tradition; the new systems for analyzing and managing risk based on this approach represents a lesser departure from convention than would a system that favors the market approach.

This victory has left some bad blood in its wake. An officer at a midwestern bank recalled that

> at the beginning [the integration] caused a fair amount of conflict as to how one should manage [new] products, whether or not market risk was something fundamentally different from credit risk and therefore not appropriately managed by traditional tools like country limits. Subsequently, this has been boiled down into a single credit equivalent and therefore jammed into the existing credit system. They are really viewed as credit products as far as risk management goes.[29]

A credit officer at a money-center bank admitted that "the hardest part has been getting traders to understand that limits are a part of banking. One way we dealt with it, early on, was to insist that they make presentations (for example, to the credit committee. Some did not do so and were sharply criticized)."[30]

According to a money-center officer, "In a way, October 19 [the 1987 stock market collapse] helped us."[31] He has suggested that traders, particularly those operating in foreign-exchange-related products, have learned about the credit risks inherent in what they do and the extent to which credit risk was being created in hedges used to cover market risk. His bank had currency swaps out to securities dealers in Japan that were due for delivery on the days following the October crash and was not sure whether the dealers were going to be around to deliver.

Resorting to Credit-Equivalent Systems

Even though the credit mentality prevailed, a new approach had to be devised to deal with the expanded scope of risk. The answer

---

[29]MNS interview, 1988.
[30]MNS interview, 1988.
[31]MNS interview, 1988.

for most banks was to create a system that would yield credit equivalents—that is, formulas that translate all different categories of risk into a single number representing the bank's exposure for the purposes of setting limits and determining capital and reserve levels. Credit equivalents allow a bank to compare, in the words of one bank economist, "a bank in Iowa with a country like Korea." The development of these formulas consumed the bulk of analysts' resources in the early to mid-1980s.

Certainly, a great deal of debate was generated in the process of devising these formulas, and each bank took a slightly different approach. Particularly vexing are qualities of risk that cannot easily be articulated in numerical terms. Country risk is one such quality. At one major bank country risk is folded in after credit equivalency has been calculated, so country risk cannot change the credit equivalency. In the opinion of a senior credit officer, other systems that use scoring techniques to measure country risk quantitatively are too complicated and cumbersome to be practical.

This approach to risk analysis has been reinforced by complementary trends in bank regulation. One banker cynically observed that new regulation helped because "people like to be told how to do these things." Yet new regulation may have confused as much as it clarified, primarily because different regulatory agencies made different demands on banks. According to a credit officer at a New York bank, the definitions of exposure for capital-adequacy purposes are not consistent with the definitions used by the Office of the Comptroller of the Currency (OCC) and the Securities and Exchange Commission (SEC). This bank's country-exposure report is shaped by the OCC's requirements, as is the management information system. Yet the OCC definitions differ from the SEC definitions, creating an inflexible MIS that cannot adapt quickly to new regulations.

Shaping Risk Assessment to Origination

Risk assessment has also been complicated by the incomplete move to portfolio and product-oriented thinking at most banks. Portfolio analysis implies a more active use of procedures such as calculating covariances between different assets and measuring asset concentration. Ideally, these calculations form the basis on which to make decisions. Yet commercial-bank management remains biased toward obligor-oriented thinking. Indeed, the decision to reduce risk indices for most transactions to a credit equivalency rather than using control mechanisms more germane to trading reflects this bias. One money-center bank officer described it this way: "The current emphasis is to organize the system by obligor for the evaluation and approval process, even though the product—and thinking in terms of product exposure—is becoming more important."

Some of the credit officers we spoke with found themselves playing to both perspectives—product-oriented and obligor-oriented—simultaneously. Often the dual mandate was settled by conducting sensitivity analyses on the portfolio but not integrating the results explicitly in the limits-setting process. One senior credit officer reported that at his bank "there is a model that can do sensitivity analyses with regard to interest rates, inflations, oil prices, etc. This has yielded interesting results, although it sparks more questions than it produces answers. We use it to further our thinking in one direction or another but make no decisions based on it."[32]

Though the credit-limits system was resurrected at most banks after the old limits system broke down, in almost every case the new system made an important concession to the trading mentality of merchant banking. Most banks established a credit limit to a particular obligor or type of obligor but then divided the limit into (1) the limit on exposure the bank is willing to hold to term, (the ceiling on loans, for example, to a particular corporation that the bank has no intention of selling down) and (2) a separate underwriting limit (the ceiling on assets that the bank is intending to sell).

Of course, banks often originate loans, most of which they hope to sell to the market. In such cases, the amount that the bank holds to term is applied against the credit limit (some banks call this the portfolio limit); the remainder falls under the underwrit-

[32]MNS interview, 1988.

ing limit (or trading limit). In other words, parts of a single asset may fall under both limits. This suggests that the credit standards applied to both limits should be the same, but some bank officers report a difference in the way each limit is perceived. One told us that credit limits "are severely controlled. We really look closely at everything which creates a term exposure. The second [underwriting limits] are much more generous."[33]

This strategy raises the difficult problem of risk control. If credit standards are less strict for underwriting exposure, line officers who originate loans might be tempted to advocate a loan as an attractive underwriting possibility rather than a term exposure. The latter would invite greater scrutiny and perhaps jeopardize the loan altogether. Hence banks also have implemented mechanisms that apply the asset to the credit limit if it cannot be liquidated after a certain period of time. A credit officer at a major midwestern bank described his system:

> Those loans that are originated to sell down on a committed basis, as opposed to a best-effort situation, are booked as an underwriting exposure. If it isn't sold in a certain amount of time, it automatically reverts to credit. Or you need [higher] approval for an extension. We do not want people booking things which in the back of their minds they are thinking of holding but taking a looser front-end approach by intending to sell. The philosophy is that ultimately someone has to hold it, so that the risk must be viewed as if you are going to hold it.[34]

Internal Controls: Limits

Even though most banks reinvented the limits system to control their new merchant-banking activities, few systems can be considered inclusive of all risks. For some products credit risk is so indirect and negligible that it is inefficient to go through the process of calculating credit equivalencies for these transactions in order to apply them against credit limits. Trading in foreign-exchange, high-quality bonds, equities, and many market instruments are therefore treated differently. Exposure limits are

[33]MNS interview, 1988.
[34]MNS interview, 1988.

calculated purely on the basis of market risk. The decision is made based on the historical behavior of the asset's price and some projection of future behavior. The banks ask themselves, How much do we want to hold given the volatility of prices and our desire to be able to sell the asset at any moment? A money-center banker put it this way:

> [For new products,] market risk is subsumed by credit risk, and they are viewed as fundamentally different from products where true market risk exists, such as trading products. There is an allocation of risk-point budget for trading functions. A risk point is an index derivative of what you might lose if interest rates change by one point in a week on so much business, so that there is a way of sizing the total market risk we are taking in investment grade assets.[35]

This last phrase is key. Credit risk is not absent from the equation; it is simply assumed to be so trivial that a limits system built around it would be inappropriate.

However, trading in assets that are below investment grade raises serious questions of credit quality, even when the bank's trading activities are similar to those in investment-grade securities. Third World loan trading offers an interesting example. In recent years some banks have decided to enter into the loan-transactions market as traders rather than simply buyers or sellers. Either system of control can be used to control this trading activity, yet most banks have opted for the conventional limits system rather than a system geared to trading. A midwestern banker told us, "When we set up the debt-trading function, we didn't manage it under the risk-point system. We gave them a credit limit for booking positions. If they take an open position on Brazilian paper, they have to do it under the Brazilian country limit."[36]

The Location of Country-Risk Analysis

As banks have diversified their international strategies, a comparable diversity is seen in their country-risk-analysis function.

[35]MNS interview, 1988.
[36]MNS interview, 1988.

Prior to the debt crisis and changes in commercial-bank strategies, country-risk-analysis units in the money-center banks strongly resembled each other. As banks have adapted to changing market realities, however, greater diversity is seen among the big banks with regard to staffing, function, and location. The pattern has changed from one of strong family resemblances to the absence of any dominant prototype.

All of the banks studied had a distinct organizational unit or subunit charged with preparing and coordinating country-risk analyses. These groups are located in several different places within the bank organization: (1) within the economics department, (2) within a separate international economics department, (3) within a separate country-risk-analysis unit, or (4) within a subunit of the international credit department.

Decentralization

Several trends can be identified within this growing diversity. First, the housing of country-risk analysis within central pools of economists located at headquarters is disappearing. Such central pools are being reduced, and at the same time their functions are being decentralized within the organization. At Bank of America, for example, international economists were located in regional offices around the world with a smaller central pool at headquarters.

This was the general thrust of a major review of central staff functions that occurred at another money-center bank. Much of the country-risk analysis was still done by local line officers with the assistance of staff economists or their own consultants. According to the head of the bank's country-risk unit, "Our economics department does put out papers, but they would not be the same kind of thing we would use, although country managers certainly might use them to prepare their reports."[37] A major New York bank also was moving in this direction. After first being separated from the central economics group (which was

[37]MNS interview, 1986.

later dissolved), international economists were moved to the credit area, where they have a matrix reporting relationship to the line units they service.

The decentralization of the international function also can be seen with regard to the analysis of exchange-rate risk. Most banks in this study separated foreign-exchange risks from other forms of international risks. The result was usually a separate economist working right on the currency trading desk and reporting to the head of that unit.

Specialization

A second discernible pattern is the creation of separate country-risk-analysis units discrete from the economics function. Several banks have had such units for some time. At one New York bank four international economists who comprise the country-risk group provide the bulk of the country-risk analysis. These economists are represented at the credit policy committee by the group's chief—a former lending officer.

Credit Imperialism

Another top U.S. bank created a country-risk management division that is separate from the bank's economics department. One distinctive characteristic of this group is its multidisciplinary composition, since, according to its head, no single discipline has a monopoly on the ability to analyze country risk. Both of these units report into the credit hierarchy.

This is indeed the third pattern—the tendency to locate the country-risk-analysis function within the credit hierarchy. According to several sources, this move has helped integrate several kinds of risk analysis (country and credit risk at a minimum) in setting country limits. It also illustrates the influential role that the credit function has retained in commercial banks. The current location of a number of risk-analysis units within the credit hierarchy suggests that if an omnibus risk-analysis unit were to emerge as a prototype, it is most likely to be within the credit hierarchy.

Support for this hypothesis emerges from the tendency in several of the banks studied to locate other specialized risk-analysis units within the credit hierarchy. For instance, one major New York bank has put its emergent industries-analysis unit within the credit hierarchy. Similarly, a major midwestern bank has created two specialty analytical groups—country-risk analysis and industry analysis—under the bank's head of credit. This was also the emergent pattern at Bankers Trust, where the rationale is that the credit function would become increasingly central to the successful execution of a merchant-banking strategy. Each of these banks are organizational hybrids, possessing units that are organized on a geographic basis and those that are functionally based.

This kind of credit imperialism seems likely to surface in other institutions. The likely emergence of credit as the bureaucratic home of an integrated risk-analysis function is reinforced by the greater influence and institutionalization of the credit function. Thus while currency forecasting and country-risk-analysis units tend to be fairly small, the credit function is typically a far larger enterprise whose head is often seated on the management committee and/or board.

The repositioning and reorganization of the risk-analysis function has also influenced the role played by bank economics departments. As country risk analysis becomes increasingly specialized and attached to the credit function, economics departments have come to play the role of stage setters for the micro forms of risk assessment. At one major midwestern bank international economists in the economics group cover the OECD economies, and their assessments are used by the country-risk analysts. The economics department also generates a macroeconomic outlook (covering, for example, oil prices, interest rates, and OECD growth) that must be approved by the credit strategy committee and that is used by the country-risk group and the rest of the bank. Its purpose is to establish uniform guidelines and assumptions for use throughout the bank.

Management Information Systems

Another measure of change is the evolving architecture of management information systems at commercial banks entering into merchant banking. In a way, MIS systems are the most concrete manifestation of the conceptual changes that have taken place in risk analysis and management. Every important decision and change in risk analysis has a counterpart in MIS, since this is the basic framework that makes these changes operational. Yet we found that in many cases operational changes lagged far behind the strategic decisions of implementation.

This conclusion is borne out by other studies. In 1988 Klynveld Peat Marwick Goerdeler conducted a study of the world's leading commercial and investment banks. In the six years leading to the October 1987 stock market crash, computer costs in the capital markets incurred by investment and commercial banks rose by an annual compound rate of 48 percent, compared to a 35 percent rate for retail brokers and a 21 percent rate for U.S. industry. Despite the costs, over 60 percent of the respondents were disappointed with their risk-management systems.[38]

Getting the Hardware Together

Most problems have arisen after banks decided that the various components of their computer systems had to be integrated. This decision was closely associated with the turn to a portfolio perspective and the tendency to look at product groups rather than obligors. In so doing, however, many banks have discovered that the computer systems for different lines of business could not communicate with each other. One credit officer's complaint: "We don't even have one system for capital markets. We have a different system for each product in some of these markets. Even worse is that there is no common identifier in these systems. We have spent a year just building links between

[38]As quoted in "International Banking: Inconsolably Incompetent," *Economist*, June 11, 1988, pp. 77–78.

the various systems in the capital markets areas, not to mention a system which would link their system to ours [the commercial banking system]."[39]

The lack of communication is an after-effect of the wild pace of innovation that took place in the earlier part of the decade. In the race to enter certain product markets, banks disposed of the need to proceed on a course that would preserve centralization, which would have slowed the bank's entry into the market and perhaps taken it out of the running altogether. According to the same credit officer, "In 1982 and 1983 the demand by the different areas was so great that the centralized area could not keep up with it. So the different areas got the authority to go out and do it on their own. Nobody even knew where every system was. We've developed a really messy situation."[40]

Getting the Software Together

The different pace of transactions has complicated matters. Systems developed to follow and control trading were designed to maximize speed, if at the expense of comprehensive data recording. This has sometimes meant that records of high-speed transactions lack information that is now considered important in the drive to integrate management information systems, adding yet another dimension to the culture clash between transaction-oriented banking and relationship-oriented banking. One banker told us that many of the early interest-rate swaps were booked without listing the domicile of the counterparties: "You didn't know what the country exposure was even if you knew how to measure the credit exposure inherent in the products."[41] Obviously, the original design of the MIS did not consider country risk—a component of credit risk—to be important.

Another problem is that different systems did not label counterparties with a common set of identifiers, which hinders the bank in tallying its exposure to a particular entity in emergencies. Although some banks in our survey claimed that they could

[39]MNS interview, 1985.
[40]MNS interview, 1988.
[41]MNS interview, 1988.

measure their total exposure to a counterparty in minutes, others admitted that they would take more than a week to completely measure exposure.

Table 3.1 presents a comparison of key management information system capabilities for some of the banks we surveyed. One outstanding quality is the very high degree of variation evident between banks, which, in turn, yielded an interesting and somewhat counterintuitive result. The best banks do not necessarily have the best systems. For example, the rating agencies regard the credit quality of bank 3's short- and long-term paper as two tiers below the quality of bank 5's short- and long-term paper. Bank 3 has been a laggard among money centers, slow to recognize its problems, slow to deal with deteriorating asset quality, slow to adapt its old systems. When that decision was finally taken, the bank simply scrapped its old system and started from scratch.

The ideal system would reduce all exposures and contingencies to a commensurate measure, cross-referenced by a series of variables including at least currency, domicile, counterparty or borrower, instrument, and maturity throughout a bank's organization. It would assimilate entries for most of the bank at least every twenty-four hours and on a close-to-real-time basis for the trading desks, and prove capable of producing a profile within a few minutes or less. One irony of the current situation is that the least prepared banks among our sample—those that have suffered the worst blows in the various lending debacles of the past decade and that in the market's judgment and sometimes their own have displayed the least imaginative management—are the institutions that through the sheer virtue of delay tend to have the best systems. The simple rule of the computer software industry prevails. He who buys last buys best.

In Closing

Commercial banks slowly are recovering the steady state that was lost to merchant banking, but this recovery has required them to undertake conceptual changes in the way they measure risk. Organizational changes have followed, although sometimes with

TABLE 3.1   *Management Information Systems—Selected Commercial Banks, 1988*

Bank	Degree of Operational Integration	Scope of Coverage[a]	Time Delay[b]	Factors in Price Changes?[c]	Measures of Concentration[d]
1	Full bank and bank holding company	All credit and trading positions	Few seconds off real time	No	Obligor, obligor's residence, point of origination, product type, currency, fixed/floating, maturity
2	Each product group has a separate system	Most but not all credit positions, few trading positions	Ranging from 24 hours to over 1 week, depending on coverage desired	No	Obligor, obligor's residence, product type, currency
3	Full bank with an interactive link to the bank holding company	All credit and trading positions	Ranging from 24 hours to 3 days, depending on coverage desired	Yes, both changes in key interest and exchange rates	Obligor, obligor's residence, product type, point of origination, currency, interest rate
4	Corporate bank only; the merchant bank has a separate system	Conventional credit exposures, plus treasury positions, plus loan asset traders	Under 10 minutes	Yes, key interest rates only	Obligor, obligor's residence, product type, currency, interest rate
5	Roughly 4 separate systems in the bank	All credit positions and some trading functions, notably treasury	Under 10 minutes within discrete systems, but days when the request crosses systems	No	Obligor, obligor's residence, product type, currency, interest rate, maturity

a. *Scope* here refers to product coverage.
b. The delay is the time lag counted from the trade or transaction.
c. Unlike the investment banks, presented later, most commercial-bank systems were not prepared to factor in interest-rate or currency exposure on the basis of significant coverage of the whole institution's activities. Coverage tended to be narrow, tied to specific trading desks.
d. *Measures of concentration* refers to the categories by which information was organized, imputed, and sorted.

trauma. The friction created by merchant banking is beginning to recede, although many of our interviewees still have grave complaints. Some of the friction will never disappear altogether. Well-managed banks depend on the adversarial relationship between those charged with maximizing returns and those charged with minimizing risks. But other frictions will have to be virtually eliminated if a bank is to remain a dynamic player in the international markets. The cultural clash between commercial- and merchant-banking activities cannot continue at its present pitch. The attendant conflict has taken heavy tolls in some banks. At some point management will have to decide that the two activities cannot be harmoniously grafted onto each other. Either they will have to be completely segregated, or the bank will have to choose one over the other. This is the battleground of the 1990s.

4

Investment Banks: The Organizational Response

In late 1985, just prior to the London big bang, we talked with Hans Joerg Rudloff, then chief executive of the London-based investment bank Credit Suisse First Boston. Before the visit we made the rounds of City banks and brokerages and heard a chorus of optimistic scenarios built on anticipated synergies and expected market expansion following deregulation, mostly from bankers whose institutions were committed to a phase of rapid growth. Mr. Rudloff provided a sober contrarian's view:

> Innovation has crippled the investment banking business because it has brought too many players into the business. The assumptions now behind market expansion are the need to maintain market share and the need to maintain a global presence. A third assumption is that deregulation will continue. This will not be the case. Excesses will fuel more regulation than ever. This idea of a laissez-faire capital markets system has never worked—not in history, not now. . . . What we're heading for is a long period of consolidation because the margins have been destroyed. Within the next two years, at least 75 percent of your current London management will be gone, and it will not be their fault. But when profits fall, people will think, the managers weren't good enough, so let's change the managers. And when that doesn't work, they'll assume that the traders weren't good enough, so they should change the traders.[1]

[1]MNS interview, 1985.

119

This view has since been justified—strikingly so. It tells the story of much of this chapter.

Growth and Shrinkage

The business cycle of the securities industry is almost as reliable as death and taxes. From roughly 1982 to 1986, in connection with a rise first in the U.S. market and subsequently in markets worldwide, the global industry boomed. Profits mushroomed, market deregulation lowered traditional barriers to entry in principal (and some not-so-principal) financial centers, ambitious plans were laid and implemented.[2] During the 1980s most firms increased their staff by 20 percent a year, and some by a good deal more. Principal arenas for expansion were New York, London, and Tokyo, but that did not preclude expansion elsewhere.

One large U.S. commercial bank we studied concluded in 1986 that investment banking would be its major source of future profits. After examining the bank's preexisting and widespread network throughout the world, management essentially decided to do everything everywhere. Dubbing this a multiproduct, multimarket strategy, expansion, particularly in brokerage, was authorized in local markets ranging from Chile to Sweden. As one officer explained at the time, "Last year [we] were ranked forty-seventh in stock-broking on the Austrian stock market and this year we're eighth. Its natural to think, 'Who cares about the Austrian stock market?,' but you put some people in, and work up to the top five, and you make the money."[3] Table 4.1 gives

[2]Even with the technical and structural changes in trading that have modified the ways brokers earn revenues and reduced the intrinsic value of Exchange membership, the price of a seat on the New York Stock Exchange remains one of the best single indicators of the robustness of the American brokerage industry. After the go-go years of the 1960s when seats hit a high of $515,000, prices began dropping in 1969 and continued to fall through 1977, two years after the deregulation of brokerage commissions, when the low of $35,000 was reached. From then on, and despite intermittent market downturns, prices rose to the historic high of $1.15 million recorded in September 1987. The most recent sale, in January 1990, saw a seat change hands at $390,000.

[3]MNS interview, 1986. The bank has subsequently withdrawn from or shrunk its dealing and market-making commitments in many of these markets. Its real franchise, instead, appears to be providing standard consumer banking services on a worldwide basis.

an approximate idea of scale for several investment banks that jumped on the global bank bandwagon. Keeping up with the competition was the paramount need, and firm after firm sought public equity or private alliances to supplement its private capital and fund expansion.

TABLE 4.1

Expansion of Investment Banks, 1975–87

Firm	Employees (% increase)			Capital (1987)	Assets (1987)
	1975–80	1980–85	1985–87		
Merrill Lynch	24%	42%	16%	$3.0 b.	$19.0 b.
Goldman Sachs	27	28	47	$3.0 b.	$42.0 b.
Drexel Burnham	25	60	25	$1.8 b.	$18.0 b.
Salomon	20	38	40	$3.0 b.	$64.0 b.

NOTE: Figures are estimates drawn from financial statements and firm sources.

As one source reasoned later, "Investment banks evolved very much like manufacturing companies. You can look at the auto industry and just take the word *auto* out and replace it with *investment bank*. In the beginning each product area would send a representative out to where the product was being sold, until enough people in that region realized they should form a discreet entity. Things carried on from there."[4] In short, decentralized operations resulted in cultures that placed a premium on initiative and innovation rather than systems and planning. Rapid expansion is difficult for anyone to handle; for the undercontrolled investment banks it proved doubly so.[5]

Trading desks began to get their firms in trouble because of the higher volumes being traded and the complicated properties of many of the new instruments. There were widely publicized losses in treasury bonds, mortgage-backed bonds, and perpetual

[4]MNS interview, 1988.
[5]Only one firm out of our group of institutions studied tried to control the pace of expansion; its executive partners ruled out expansion beyond the limit of the firm's retained earnings.

floating-rate notes, among a host of others. More hidden losses were suspected and potential losses feared.[6] One London-based source commented bitterly,

> The real question is why are there so many gimmicks. Those cheaper borrowings—you have borrowers who have no idea what they're doing. New York money managers have a lot of pride in the aggressive way they manage money, in their ability to cut the borrowing costs right now. They are playing around with their balance sheets day in and day out to save ten or twenty basis points here or there, and they are playing around in a very big way. To save twenty basis points now, a treasurer will risk 100 basis points in the future.[7]

By 1987 trading revenues were dropping, even before the October market break. *Investment Dealers Digest* reported that Wall Street firms generated $2.0 billion of revenue from underwriting all types of domestic securities in 1987, over 50 percent off the 1986 figure of $5.1 billion. Traditional sources of brokerage revenue—trading commissions and spreads on underwritings—became ever less remunerative, with the overall effect of forcing traders to risk larger sums in order to gain roughly the same amount. Deregulation, increased competition from commercial banks and previously excluded foreign firms (especially the Japanese), and ever larger sums of capital allocated to capital-markets activity all contributed to greatly aggravating the normal industry cycle. In the simplest terms, the supply of traders continued to build and demand continued to shrink, all of which promoted overtrading and risk taking.

To some degree the behavior of firms reflected their compensa-

---

[6]In 1987 we talked briefly with a number of our sources in both commercial and investment banks. Widely voiced at the time was the general suspicion that major banks involved in the interest-rate swaps market had experienced losses connected with counterparty defaults, none of which had been publicly revealed or tested in court. Thus, many respondents concluded that losses had been buried either to protect the reputation of a swiftly growing market or because the bank intermediaries were so uncertain of their legal documentation they preferred not to test it. In mid-1986 interviews we conducted at the Federal Reserve Bank of New York left it clear that a major source of anxiety was the imbalance between buyers (too many) and sellers (too few and unidentified) in the foreign-exchange options market. Since the seller's risk is potentially infinite, unease on the part of the national lender of last resort was appropriate.

[7]MNS interview, 1987.

tion incentive structures, and a comparative note is useful here. At the end of 1986 the average broker's payout rate in the United States was 41 percent. On January 1, 1988, Merrill Lynch reduced its payout rate to 36 percent and would not be followed by its competitor firms for another twelve months. In the meantime, the average payout rate among the big four Japanese securities houses was 10 percent. Return-on-equity figures reflect these differences.

Following the 1987 market break, Jon Moynihan of First Manhattan Consulting Group estimated the costs of an untraded treasury bond portfolio held from 1982 through 1986, as compared to real bond department profits, and found them roughly equal. Looking at this result, several commentators on the financial scene suggested that the impressive performance of Wall Street's trading desks during the 1980s was simply an artifact of generally rising values and not necessarily evidence that traders had any very good idea of what they were doing.

From Trading to Investment Banking: The Return of Overend Gurney?[8]

As revenue from the trading desk fell off, revenue from corporate-finance activities largely replaced it, a phenomenon dating

[8]An established and successful bill discount house active in London during the previous century "whose name had become a byword for strength and integrity," the firm of Overend Gurney underwent a change of senior partners and a tremendous expansion and diversification of business away from its conventional activity of discounting bills. By 1860 the firm was losing money from its speculations in grain, iron production, shipbuilding, shipping, and railroad finance. Nevertheless, little understanding the firm's business, the public bought eagerly when the house became a public limited liability company in July 1865. The bubble was pricked less than a year later, and the crisis that followed brought widespread failure in the financial system, a Bank of England discount rate of 10 percent, and suspension of the Bank Act. Contemporaries were scathing. Hyndman remarked that the firm's new managers were "sapient nincompoops" while the eminent Bagehot judged, "These losses were made in a manner so reckless and so foolish that one would think a child who had lent money in the City of London would have lent it better." See G. A. Fletcher, *The Discount Houses in London* (London: Macmillan, 1976), H. M. Hyndman, *Commercial Crises of the Nineteenth Century* (New York: Augustus M. Kelley, 1967 [reprint]), and Walter Bagehot, *Lombard Street: A Description of the Money Market*, (Homewood, Ill.: R.D. Irwin, 1962).

roughly from late 1986 through 1989, with a downturn becoming evident in the latter part of that year. Many of the contextual and organizational variables were the same: euphoria continued to characterize the market; innovations were common, although oriented more toward packaging credit risk; rapid expansion, organizational strains, and overworked systems continued to be the status quo. While trading desks continued to handle huge daily sums in volatile markets, investment bankers began to bet their firm's capital in restructurings, leveraged buyouts, and merchant banking.

Despite the 1987 stock market break, LBO operations slowed only temporarily. In mid-1988 activities were taking place on a tremendous scale. In June of that year one source counted over $10 billion invested in U.S. LBO funds,[9] yielding $100 billion as the sum either invested or available for investment according to a representative leverage ratio of ten to one. Business was spreading to London and Continental financial centers, although in these more phlegmatic markets it rarely reached the levels of activity sustained in the United States.

Market euphoria assisted the decoupling of investment values from the underlying market prices. As star fund manager George Soros would later observe,

> Valuation is a positive act that makes an impact on the course of events. Monetary and real phenomena are connected in a reflexive fashion; that is, they influence each other mutually. The reflexive relationship manifests itself most clearly in the use and abuse of credit. Loans are based on the lender's estimation of the borrower's ability to service his debt. The valuation of the collateral is supposed to be independent of the act of lending; but in actual fact the act of lending can affect the value of collateral. This is true of the individual case and of the economy as a whole.[10]

The decoupling of values and prices did not pass unobserved. The 1987 market break left the aggregate market roughly a

[9]"America's Capital Markets Survey," *Economist*, June 11, 1988, pp. 9–10.
[10]George Soros, *Reading the Mind of the Market* (New York: Simon & Schuster, 1988), pp. 17–18.

quarter below its highs for the year, yet LBO-related purchase prices failed to reflect the discount, a phenomenon provoking Peter Solomon, then cohead of Shearson Lehman's investment banking department, to remark, "Prices were down and values apparently did not change. This is something nobody would have expected."[11]

Apart from the considerable controversy surrounding the figure of Michael Milken and the LBO activities of his firm Drexel Burnham Lambert, there were contrarians who criticized the business as such. Ace Greenburg, head of the respected firm Bear Stearns, was widely cited as a skeptic who defined merchant banking as "buying an unlisted and unregistered security in a business you know absolutely nothing about," and described LBO-related bridge loans as "a form of suicide." In this regard Bear Stearns was one of the first investment banks to set up a specialized "troubled corporate debt" unit that earned tremendous returns by selectively making limited investments in securities of leveraged firms that were either in chapter 11 bankruptcy proceedings or headed that way—essentially, making money shorting the LBO market.

Partial adjustments began to be seen in 1989 and 1990 as liquidity fell off drastically in the secondary market for junk bonds, and the stock market became considerably more attuned to takeover stocks that were, during market setbacks, marked down more than the market as a whole. By then, many market participants had liquidated their holdings,[12] but more than one

---

[11]As quoted in "America's Capital Markets survey," *Economist*, June 11, 1988, pp. 9–10.

[12]Alan Abelson's column in *Barron's*, June 27, 1988, pp. 1ff., contains a characteristically caustic analysis of the initial public offering (IPO) of a nationwide chain of clinical laboratories called National Health Laboratories, previously part of the Revlon cosmetics group acquired by Ronald Perelman in a leveraged buyout. The IPO consisted of a sale of 9 percent of NHL's equity to be underwritten by Drexel Burnham Lambert. The remaining 91 percent of equity was to be controlled by Mr. Perelman's holding company, MacAndrews & Forbes. The 9 percent was offered at $126 million and on the strength of rapid expansion was earning around thirty-six cents per share. Abelson pointed out that total stockholder's equity of $308 million included intangible assets of $200 million, assets arising from the Revlon LBO. Postoffering tangible book value was estimated at forty-eight cents per share, nearly all of which would arise from the proceeds of the offering itself. Without the offering, tangible book value was a negative forty-six cents per share (such was the debt load of the company). The proceeds of the offering were

firm was caught by events, holding substantial and untradeable positions.

Although we have not seen anything on a scale to compare with the debacle of London's Overend Gurney, the cyclical downturn is not complete.[13] It is probably not mistaken to assume that the Federal Reserve Bank's efforts to manage an economic slowdown without provoking a recession are at least partially influenced by the pervasiveness of high-interest-rate debt throughout the corporate sector.

Managing the Cycle: What the Investment Banks Did

The large U.S. and European investment banks were and are traders first and bankers second. Not only is firm strategy driven by the up-and-down cycle of the markets, but it tends to mean one thing on the way up and another thing altogether on the way down.

On the up side, management is a matter of organizing territory and controlling greed—getting people to give up territory for the good of the firm. The firm's expansion is driven by its outermost points—a money-market salesperson who discovers a niche to fill in Belgian commercial paper or a foreign-exchange trader who sees opportunities in a currency new to the bank. Strategy becomes an after-the-fact story, useful in explaining the firm to outsiders or teaching it to new employees. As one source observed in the midst of the bull market phase, "Investment banks operate in an inductive rather than a deductive way, and this is actually characteristic of trading businesses as a whole. You

---

intended to retire debt (a note held by MacAndrews & Forbes), which, in turn, had been originally issued to meet payment of a dividend of $175 million to Mr. Perelman, via a corporate proxy. Despite the offering, Abelson estimated that NHL would continue to be in debt to MacAndrews & Forbes for another $40 million.

[13]This section was written prior to the bankruptcy of Drexel Burnham Lambert, which serves quite well as the contemporary incarnation of Overend Gurney. In this case, however, the collapse of the house does not, in our opinion, coincide with the low point of the market. That remains ahead of us.

know what you should be doing without knowing necessarily why you should be doing it."[14]

In a bear market, management becomes a matter of finding out what is going on, controlling against losses, controlling risk, and controlling costs (often by firing staff). The systems people, credit officers, and even controllers take on greater influence. Strategy becomes a real enterprise, at least according to the sense in which it is commonly understood. Having suffered setbacks, the desire to pinpoint where the firm stands acquires urgency. Strategy becomes a matter of assessing markets, evaluating business lines, and, it is hoped, charting a recovery.

We first researched investment banks in 1985 and 1986 and in the process found virtually no strategic originality. The dominant story foresaw global trading principally centered in New York, London, and Tokyo, with expanding business in smaller regional centers, all being serviced by ten to fifteen large investment banks that would become increasingly sophisticated at managing twenty-four hour trading positions and executing cross-border corporate finance and banking transactions. The number of firms, by contrast, that critically examined regulatory and economic changes on a market-by-market basis, guiding themselves accordingly, could be counted on one hand with fingers left over. These firms differed sharply from the herd. They also managed to avoid losing a lot of money.

Growing Internationally

Every bank we studied in the bull market phase already possessed well-established businesses in New York and London and had recently opened or expanded operations in Tokyo. Most developed around a full-service approach, with operations reflecting the characteristics of local markets. The focus of the three principal centers, however, was complemented by a widespread international presence that typically saw each bank involved in not less than fifty countries, at least in the sense of being exposed to meaningful credit or market risk. Incremental expansion favored

[14]MNS interview, 1986.

the creation and merchandising of new capital-markets products, rather than the more geography-tied and relationship-centered activities of advising corporations, effecting restructurings, or executing acquisitions.

Organizing around Products

The banks' first pass at growing their international business involved reorganizing traditional management structures. Having grown from key bank-client relationships, more often than not these reflected geographic expansion around one or a handful of key personalities (our man in Sydney). What was needed instead was a bankwide organization around product lines, such as foreign exchange (major currency, minor currency), corporate bonds, government bonds, structured financings, bond/equity hybrids, and so on, essentially fitting the bank to the logic of local origination and innovation but international selling of specialized products. "Our world has become a pure capital markets world," claimed one source. "We divide our clients into 'money junkies' and 'good girls'—the first award us business strictly on price. They're always in the market, borrowing, refunding, or fine tuning. The second group will occasionally give us business on the strength of a relationship, and in any case is much less present in the market."[15]

As a by-product, the nearly universal shift to product-line organizations encouraged the creation of product-innovation groups—in-house think tanks often staffed with ex-business school finance professors, ex-physicists, and other higher maths hired away at multiples of their old salaries strictly for the purpose of coming up with new wrinkles for salespeople who, in turn, had to feed the borrowers who, in turn, were nearly always in the market. Interesting as a phenomenon, these groups were rarely successful in practice. "Our group just kind of evolved and then kind of un-evolved, all in about two years,"[16] observed one source. Even if their jobs changed, for the most

[15]MNS interview, 1986.
[16]MNS interview, 1987.

part, the higher maths stayed on. The new products kept getting more complicated.

The product range offered by banks mushroomed. At one time a U.S. corporation would have planned a borrowing, prepared an SEC registration filing with its investment banker, and gone to market in a matter of months. The new market consisted of corporations with multiple borrowing horizons that, with internal staff, had prepared a series of approved registrations to cover all possibilities. When a currency opportunity or interest-rate window appeared, the borrower went to market with an investment bank, preferably one prepared to take the entire amount on its books at time of issue (later to feed it out), all in under thirty minutes.

The banks had to have more capital. Not only was there expansion to fund and "bought" deals to trade, but winning business increasingly came to depend on warehousing. Innovation itself was not sufficient, as ideas were nearly as fungible as money, and a bank had to bring something more to the table. In the mid-1980s investment banks were nearly exclusively involved in the swaps market as arrangers—bringing two counterparties together, taking a fee, and accepting little or no credit risk. By late 1986 most banks had substantial swap and option books of positions they themselves were carrying and could lay off or open up to a potential borrower. Foreign exchange developed from a business where positions lasting more than one month were rare, to a business where investment banks were holding and managing positions going out ten years. Bank risk and bank profits rose together.

Loosening Credit Standards

Recognizing higher risks, banks moved to formalize their internal processes for introducing products. In many cases this meant tightened scrutiny before a new product could be sold to a potential client. In some cases product-review circles were created. Typically consisting of a senior director, a credit officer, a trader, a representative from the bank's funding side, and a salesperson, these groups analyzed the risk of new products, sometimes test-ing them against various scenarios, before they left the bank.

The task of maintaining risk discipline, already strained by expansion and innovation, was complicated by negative market trends. By the middle of 1986 the forces of increased competition and a falling off in the pace of borrowing, particularly by quality sovereign borrowers, began to encourage a general weakening in credit barriers. Investment banks were pushed to dilute their internal standards just as the commercial banks had been.

One case illustrates both the process and the pace. In 1985 one investment bank credit officer portrayed his bank's swap business primarily as one of arranging deals between counterparties rated single A or better. By 1986 his bank ran a substantial swap port-folio and drew the line at BB counterparties.[17] A year later one of the bank's most profitable growth areas was secondary-market trading in the securitized loans of Third World countries, an activity involving substantial temporary positions in a manifestly illiquid market, and had begun to accept some Mexican and Latin American banks as counterparties on long-term foreign-ex-change commitments. The same credit officer could still claim with pride that his bank had taken no credit losses (they had experienced defaults, but in each case the collateral held up), but the strain was visible.

Following the deterioration of sovereign lending came the boom in buyout-related financing and a rapid acceleration in what was up until that time relatively limited pools of financial activity in junk bonds. The deterioration of borrower credit

---

[17]Most credit-rating agencies use substantially similar letter-grade rating systems. Ac-cording to Moody's, A-rated bonds "possess many favorable investment attributes and are to be considered as upper medium grade obligations. Factors giving security to princi-pal and interest are considered adequate but elements may be present which suggest a susceptibility to impairment sometime in the future." *Moody's Bond Record* 57 (4) (April 1990): 1. Standard & Poor's defines the BB bond this way: "Debt rated 'BB,' 'B,' 'CC,' and 'C' is regarded as having predominantly speculative characteristics with respect to capac-ity to pay interest and repay principal. 'BB' indicates the least degree of speculation and 'C' the highest. While such debt will likely have some quality and protective characteris-tics, these are outweighed by large uncertainties or major exposures to adverse conditions. . . . Debt rated 'BB' has less near-term vulnerability to default than other speculative issues. However, it faces major ongoing uncertainties or exposure to adverse business, financial, or economic conditions, which could lead to inadequate capacity to meet timely interest and principal payments." *S&P's High Yield Quarterly* 2 (1) (March 15, 1990): 72.

moved forward a step as lower-credit-quality corporate borrowers exploited a new access to securities markets. A familiar, but often forgotten, pattern was reasserting itself.

The cycle was slowed by the 1987 market break, giving credit departments and back offices a chance to regain their footing. Fearing unpredictable markets, borrowers shifted toward conventional instruments that investors purchased more readily for the same reason. The flow of new products slowed, and momentum within the banks began to shift from traders and capital-markets specialists. Managing for bear market conditions began to come forward.

Improving Controls

In 1988, talking with a capital-markets specialist at the Federal Reserve Bank of New York, we received the supervisory community's bottom-line definition of adequate internal-risk control: "An institution, whether it's a commercial bank or an investment bank, must know its exposure to each counterparty at all times, on a consolidated basis and in real time. How many institutions can do this?"[18] As we subsequently discovered, not one. Whether this gap reflects the traditional distance between the supervisor's trust (to worry, in the public interest) and the banker's job (to make money, in the shareholder's interest) or something more seriously amiss, the real improvements that were instituted at the initiative of the banks themselves should not be discounted.

As was observed in chapter 2 meaningful changes have come in basically four areas: instituting formal controls over product introduction, strengthening credit apparatus, improving management information systems, and improving formal limits monitoring. Here we focus on improvement made in the latter two areas.

Improving Management Information Systems

"A good management information system is the sine qua non of risk management," according to one investment banker. "With-

18MNS interview, 1988.

out this, one cannot have an effective risk management system."[19] The purpose of an MIS is to keep management informed of essential business developments. In a banking environment characterized predominantly by trading activities in volatile markets, the system must capture all the firm's exposures, wherever they are undertaken, as close to real market time as possible. When a bank has traders active twenty-four hours out of twenty-four, the system must function in a globally integrated way with limited down time. When the products that a bank trades are frequently unbundled and retailored to suit the occasion, the system must not only identify generic product types but provide close to real-time reporting of discrete product constituents—interest rates, exchange rates, option features, maturities, and so forth.

In 1980 most investment banks were operating with systems primarily geared to the recording of trades to suit settlement responsibilities, provide periodic (daily, or more likely weekly) position reports, and provide a running profit-and-loss evaluation of key trading and sales desks. Thus the firm could track its activity on conventional products, without a pressing need to expand its control beyond two, or perhaps three, time zones and without regard for unbundling, which, in any case, did not reflect actual markets.

By 1988 virtually all investment bank systems had been revised, some more so than others. The typical bank prepared a system revision in late 1985 or early 1986 that from the outset took some account of the requirements mentioned above. The period of testing and implementing the system design lasted between three and four years, with the system applied first to the bank's most credit-sensitive activities, typically commercial and Eurocommercial paper. A typical back-end problem tackled once the system was up for most of the bank's activities was how to feed data from distant zones into the central offices system in a way that allowed management to act on it. Some time-zone problems may turn out to be insuperable.

"We feed in our Tokyo input [to New York] overnight," ex-

---

[19]MNS interview, 1988.

plained one credit officer. "Our clearing and settling area gets the feed on a real-time basis from everywhere. When we [credit] get the feed, it may be as much as twenty-four or as little as two hours old, just depending on when we get it. . . . That's one of the things we're working on. One of the problems, however, is that there's not much you can do when you get it. Tokyo's closed, after all. I mean, you can tell your traders in London to hold off and tell your traders here the same, but that's about it."[20] Table 4.2 shows the key properties of a restructured management information system in 1988. It is representative, in that our survey showed that nearly all the institutions we watched reached roughly similar positions with similar results.

System improvements by themselves mean relatively little unless they are supplemented by a fairly rigorous limits-control procedure that standardizes rules for how the bank counts its exposure, and by a management philosophy that respects and enforces the bank's periodic need to refuse deals. The latter, like strategy itself, tends to wax and wane with market cycles. Limits-control procedures, however, have improved fairly steadily.

Improving Formal Limits Monitoring

Adapting analytical approaches defined in the late 1970s to the late 1980s market environment consisted basically of expanding to include new products and altering definitions of risk, primarily to take account of greatly increased volatility in certain markets. In the early 1980s most investment banks were not involved with either the trading of low-credit-quality loans or long-term foreign-exchange contracts. Including a new product in a bank's limits system necessarily places upper limits on its activity, since it applies some portion of the bank's capital against the exposure. Capital, of course, is itself a variable number, depending on the institution's overall capital leverage, but it is a scarce and jealously guarded resource.

Traders across the board prefer markets with significant volatility since this yields profit opportunities. The problem for

[20]MNS interview, 1988.

TABLE 4.2

Management Information Systems: A Representative Investment/Merchant Bank, 1988

Degree of Operational Integration[a]	Scope of Coverage[b]	Time Delay[c]	Factors in Price Changes[d]	Measures of Concentration[e]
Roughly 80% of the bank's activities, organized globally by product group	Every credit exposure, including all trading positions	5 seconds off real time for the slowest feed to reach the bank; internal dissemination thereafter to interested departments was slower (although rarely more than 24 hours)	Interest and exchange rates	Obligor, obligor's residence, product type, point of origination, currency, maturity, fixed/floating type collateral

a. The generally professed goal was to gradually expand to 100 percent, but most institutions felt comfortable with the established networks.
b. *Scope* here refers to product coverage.
c. The delay is the time lag counted from the trade or transaction. In the event of trouble, most banks were in a position to order a fire drill, which gathered all relevant exposure information by counterparty within a minute of real time. Gathering the same information by geographic market, in most cases, took longer and was harder to do. For full coverage, delay might be a matter of hours; for 90 percent coverage, delay might be a matter of fifteen minutes.
d. The bank's goal was to mount a system that could quickly present an overall picture of its interest-rate or currency exposure. The system applied to contracts, collateral, and trades that were subject to changing rates and needed to be marked to market.
e. *Measures of concentration* refers to the categories by which information was organized, inputed, and sorted.

their credit counterparts is to keep matters in hand, especially when a position has meaningful term exposure. The need to control spot foreign-exchange trading is fundamentally limited and, in any case, best applied directly by the trader who is in and out of the market according to basic rules that guide the bank's activity. The need to control a long-term forward contract, however, is a credit question, complicated by volatility that may require more intensive monitoring, a larger capital allocation, more frequent marking to market, or other measures. By 1988 a typical limits-control system reflected these needs. An example is produced in table 4.3.

That controls have been improved is comforting for those whose job it is to worry about systemic soundness and stability. The measures taken by the banks at their own initiative represent the first and most important line of defense in maintaining sound banking and trading conditions. Market shocks will inevitably occur; how institutions cope is critical. Banking is one industry where firefighting, by necessity, means getting the firefighters in place before anything happens. In the best of all worlds they will never be used.

Weak Links

Even with improvements, however, some points of stress remain uncovered.

The Problem of the Global Book

In 1985 hubris tempted bankers to pronounce routinely on the inevitability of global markets and global trading. In retrospect, relatively few markets are truly global. Foreign exchange is one; related futures and options contracts are becoming so as the various exchanges knit their capabilities across time zones. Government bonds and some corporate bonds and equities are underwritten and traded in several markets, but the bulk of activity in bonds, equities, hybrids, swaps, commercial paper, and notes remains attached in a conventional way to principal markets.

TABLE 4.3

What's Counted in Internal Limits: A Representative Investment/Merchant Banking System, 1988

Currency and Interest-Rate Swaps	Repurchase Agreements and Reverse Repos	Futures and Options	Long-Dated Forward Contracts	Trading Positions in:			
				CDs[a]	CP[b]	BAs[c]	LDC Loans[d]
3% of notional amount per annum	5% of agreement value	Initial margin is equal to total estimated possible market move; on in-the-money contracts the margin is a 1-day limit move	15% of face value	100%	100%	100%	Total purchase value

a. Certificates of deposit.
b. Commercial paper.
c. Bankers' acceptances.
d. Loans to less developed countries traded in the over-the-counter secondary market.

With activities that are global, however, the problem of actually constructing a global book, passing it, hedging it, and controlling the risk remains a challenge. Progress varies by bank, and there are ragged edges between time zones. Risk control is difficult. Positions taken in one market cannot necessarily be well managed in another when the first market is closed and the book has moved on. For most of our sources this constituted an important object of their energies.

The Problem of Liquidity

The risk of sudden and unexpected illiquidity, particularly as it might affect a relatively new market and untested products, remains serious. The improvements mentioned above do not incorporate this risk, in part because the variable is so difficult to visualize. "Liquidity cannot be measured, not even defined," observed one source at the Federal Reserve Bank of New York,[21] "but even if it's somewhat mysterious, it needs to be worried about." The interim solution appears to rest with banks' willingness to thoroughly prepare before launching a new product or engaging in a new activity.

Quite clearly the presence of liquidity, particularly in a new market, rests on the confidence of investors and intermediaries that the market is balanced, reasonably transparent, and not rigged. The lack of all three qualities in some sectors of the Euromarket has resulted in that market's current difficulties. That those difficulties are linked to overcapacity and high levels of competition is clear. There is no conclusion to be drawn except that liquidity will continue to be an intermittent problem characterizing many markets and occasionally a significant threat to some in moments of stress.

As the Cross Committee pointed out, the firms themselves cannot be expected to shoulder the responsibility for market soundness. As price takers, firms should at most be expected to make studied decisions about which markets they wish to participate in and which they prefer to avoid. Those who commit them-

[21]MNS interview, 1988.

selves strategically for the long term know well that their self-interest lies in bringing reasonably balanced deals, backed by market-making commitments. Inevitably Gresham's law will take effect when a flush of bad business renders difficult the conduct of good business. The strength of a serious firm lies in its ability and willingness to turn down bad business.

Such self-discipline in the securities and banking industry is commonly manifested, although perhaps not frequently in public view. It varies widely within firms, between firms, and between sectors of the banking industry, and it also varies with the up and down cycles characterizing markets and sectors.

The history surrounding lenders of last resort shows that the liquidity risk should not be eliminated, especially not by public authorities, since doing so presents market participants with an irresistible one-way bet. The long-term consequences of that approach can be seen in many areas, not least the U.S. thrift industry.

This process of excess and partial correction is carried out by and within the firms themselves. We believe the process is unfinished and will continue. The risk of shock and collapse is always present. Although banks and securities firms have overextended themselves in this period, back-end behavior of retrenchment, consolidation, and the rebuilding of internal controls is evident everywhere. The banks remain overextended to some degree and the system continues to manifest signs of strain, but we believe the riskiest passages have been completed, with market breaks but without widespread market collapse. The imperative now is not to reverse the process of correction.

5

Conclusion

In a reflective moment, one source remarked to us that there is really very little novelty in finance generally, and that this truth holds good for situations as well as instruments. As we wrote this book, we were drawn again and again to that comment, finding it apt from many viewpoints. Given that this book purports to be about innovations, the admission may sound odd. Nevertheless, the situation in which we find ourselves is recognizable as a recurrent phase in the history of both national and international financial markets; the risks and the behavior of participants can also be recognized and reasoned about in terms of analogy. Although the density, complexity, and scale of relationships woven by current actors between markets and institutions may have attained new levels, the balance between these problems and our capacity to deal with them may be no more challenging than has been the case for others in similar times.

The circumstances of previous periods of financial excess and correction has been examined by other writers, and we can do readers a favor by referring them onward.[1] It may be useful to dwell on three large perplexities characterizing the immediate context—problems that form the backdrop to this essay.

---

[1] A great deal of material can be found in Charles Kindleberger's small but excellent *Manias, Panics and Crashes: A History of Financial Crises* (New York: Basic Books, 1978). The first three chapters of Charles Mackay's older (1841) *Extraordinary Popular Delusions and the Madness of Crowds* (New York: Harmony, 1980) are also entertaining.

First, the nature of money itself has changed. It has become protean and more abundant over the last two decades as a direct consequence of other factors: the creation of new types of money and near money, the increased ease of money transmission and money's greater resultant fungibility, and the diffusion beyond deposit-taking banks of the ability to create money by creating credit. Being more plastic, money is less susceptible to definition and control. The original definition of high-powered money coined by Milton Friedman and Anna Schwartz, and which formed a cornerstone of modern monetary theory, is so inapplicable to contemporary financial reality that one contemporary writer, frustrated in trying to actually pinpoint high-powered money in contemporary markets, spoofed the whole idea. High-powered money, he thought, might best be defined as "that portion of the banks' funding requirements that they have been unable at the close of day to get out of the type of liabilities that the Fed requires them to keep as a reserve."[2]

With so difficult a variable as centerpiece, monetary restraint as a policy of central banks has become more easily circumvented—loose and elastic. The entities that it affects also have changed, with financial institutions bearing less and the final bidders for credit—households and businesses—bearing more.

The time required for credit restraint to be felt in the behavior of actors also has lengthened. "It was far easier in the past to conduct monetary policy effectively than it is today," observed Henry Kaufman while still at Salomon Brothers. "In the new financial world, more entities become substantial debtors even in periods of restraint, because under the spread banking approach—the quick raising of rates of return on assets as the cost of liabilities rises to financial intermediaries—final demanders of credit boost the price of credit, and the innovative suppliers are able to satisfy them until interest costs and associated risks become too high for borrowers."[3] A key policy tool has been rendered less viable, placing more weight on fiscal policy. This cannot be considered a positive development, since the relative

[2]Martin Mayer, "The Settlements Revolution," *Institutional Investor* (April 1982).
[3]Henry Kaufman, *The Federal Reserve and the Changing Financial Markets* (Salomon Brothers Bond Market Research, 1986), pp. 3–4.

fiscal irresponsibility of most congresses and parliaments at the moment is indisputably evident.

Second, and frequently discussed in this book, the risk tenor of institutions and the system as a whole has ratcheted upward. Easing it down again is tricky, largely because the system is composed of interdependent segments—chess rather than checkers, as one source put it—that form the weft of the financial system. In a well-crafted essay, Gerald Corrigan, president of the Federal Reserve Bank of New York, stated the situation this way:

> Access to the securities markets for private borrowers does not occur in a vacuum; it is earned and importantly so through banking relationships. Moreover, securities markets are not particularly well-equipped for coping with severe liquidity strains or "workout" problems for individual borrowers. It is primarily for these reasons that bank intermediaries often provide the backup facilities that permit the securities markets to function as they do. . . . Regardless of the precise way in which credit is extended, the stability of the system requires that the credit decision-making process be rigorous and objective and that it be able to screen out, or at least isolate, bad credits while at the same time reasonably insuring that economic agents with legitimate credit and liquidity needs have the capacity to borrow at reasonable costs.[4]

It is precisely the risk-transforming, -passing, and -modifying qualities of these products that have altered both the task of risk evaluation and the way institutions make their credit decisions. For the interim, these products have jeopardized the structure as a whole, at least until it has time to assimilate the consequences of these transactions. At the same time, interdependence has increased rather than diminished. Institutions outside traditional regulatory networks step forward as risk takers; institutions within the networks devote considerable ingenuity and time to circumventing them; the networks themselves are fragmented and discrete, promoting the impulse for "everyone to get into everyone else's business."

The deconstruction of the credit pyramid, even in the partial

[4]E. Gerald Corrigan, *Financial Market Structure: A Longer View* (New York: Federal Reserve Bank of New York, 1987), p. 18.

and marginal sense implied by the goal of achieving a sounder but lower overall gearing, will probably entail widespread and hurtful consequences—preferable only to greater future dangers. Distributing those will involve distasteful political choices, which, being difficult, may be shirked by those best suited to take them. Throwing the political problem onto the regulatory institutions themselves, perhaps in the form of a politicized and too relaxed policy of credit availability, is a present danger.

Third, we perceive a number of political risks ahead for the key supervisory and central banking authorities in OECD nations. The mixing of supervisory issues with trade issues is one possibility; politicized credit policy is certainly another. Central banks have varying degrees of legal and institutional independence from their respective executive governments. Some are more fragile than others. The governor of the Bank of England is recognized as an agent of the Chancellor of the Exchequer. His political clout resides in his persuasiveness and the prestige of his position. As is widely appreciated, the German Bundesbank represents the other extreme, with its independence guaranteed by both constitutional and other juridical supports. For many supervisory officials, however, the husbandry of independence that allows meaningful action will be a timely priority.

There is deep skepticism on the part of many about the continued viability of international cooperation among supervisory authorities, particularly when it conflicts with the prerogatives of national governments. As Susan Strange has argued persuasively, "Surely the whole experience of the European Community has shown that playing 'grandmother's footsteps' with the nation state is no easy game. For as soon as national autonomy and freedom of action are seriously threatened, the pace of 'supranational' decision-making slows to a crawl, and resistance, instead of weakening, begins to harden."[5] International cooperation is essential in the tasks ahead, both in higher-level policy formation and in the more mundane tasks of devising internationally comparable systems for gathering pertinent information. The permeable nature of national market systems and ease of regulatory "arbitrage" requires deliberate cooperation.

[5]Susan Strange, *Casino Capitalism* (Oxford: Basil Blackwell, 1986), p. 151.

References

"America's Capital Markets Survey." *Economist*, June 11, 1988, 9–10.

Bagehot, Walter. *Lombard Street: A Description of the Money Market.* Homewood, Ill.: R. D. Irwin, 1962.

Bank for International Settlements. *International Convergence of Capital Measurement and Capital Standards.* Basle: BIS Committee on Banking Regulations and Supervisory Practices, July 1988, BS/88/62e.

———. *Recent Innovations in International Banking.* Basle: BIS, April 1986.

Bartlett, Sarah. "Bankers Trust Could Beat the Street at Its Own Game." *Business Week*, April 4, 1988, 87.

Bennett, Robert A. "Sanford's New Banking Vision." *New York Times,* March 17, 1985, sec. 3, 1.

Bentson, George, Gerald Hanweck, and David Humphrey. "Scales Economies in Banking: A Restructuring and Reassessment." *Journal of Money, Credit, and Banking* 14 (1982): 435–36.

Corrigan, E. Gerald. *Financial Market Structure: A Longer View.* New York: Federal Reserve Bank of New York, 1987.

Dickson, Martin. "When Relations Are Put to the Test." *Financial Times,* Jan. 7, 1988, 19.

Feldstein, Martin. "Strengthening the American Financial System." In Giacomo Luciani, *La Finanza Americana Fra Euforia e Crisi.* Milan: Fondazione Olivetti, 1989.

Fidler, Stephen, and Claire Pearson. "Six Dealers Drop Subordinated FRNS." *Financial Times,* March 15, 1988, 34.

Fletcher, G. A. *The Discount Houses in London.* London: Macmillan, 1976.

Gilligan, Thomas, Michael Smirlock, and William Marshall. "Scale and Scope Economies in the Multi-Product Banking Firm." *Journal of Monetary Economics* 13 (1984): 393–405.

Guenther, Robert. "Investment Bankers Lose Out in Chase Reorganization." *Wall Street Journal,* May 4, 1988, 26.

———. "Morgan's Adviser Role in Takeover Fight Strains Relationship with an Old Client." *Wall Street Journal,* April 13, 1988, p. 6.

Hanley, Thomas, James Rosenberg, Carla D'Arista, Neil Mitchell, and Jay Rodin. *A Review of Bank Performance.* Salomon Brothers, April 1985.

147

————. *A Review of Bank Performance.* Salomon Brothers, April 1987.

Heimann, John. *International Capital Markets: Issues and Risks.* Paris: Institut d'Études Bancaires et Financières, 1987.

Humphrey, David. "Cost Dispersion and the Measurement of Economies in Banking." *Economic Review* 73(3) (May/June 1987): 24–38.

Hyndman, H. M. *Commercial Crises of the Nineteenth Century.* New York: Augustus M. Kelley, 1967 [reprint].

"Institutional Investor." *Bank Letter,* April 18, 1988, 5.

"International Banking: Inconsolably Incompetent." *Economist,* June 11, 1988, 77–78.

Kaufman, Henry. *The Federal Reserve and the Changing Financial Markets.* New York: Salomon Brothers Bond Market Research, 1986.

Keynes, John Maynard. *The General Theory of Employment, Interest and Money.* New York: Harcourt Brace Jovanovich, 1964.

Kindleberger, Charles. *Manias, Panics and Crashes.* New York: Basic Books, 1978.

"Learning to Manage." *Economist,* June 25, 1988, 10.

Lee, Elliott D. "Salomon Finds That There Are Pitfalls When Investing in Unfamiliar Markets." *Wall Street Journal,* June 14, 1988, 7.

Lewis, Michael. *Liar's Poker.* New York: Norton, 1989.

Liebowitz, Martin. *Vistas for Innovation.* Salomon Brothers, November 1981.

Mackay, Charles. *Extraordinary Popular Delusions and the Madness of Crowds.* New York: Harmony, 1980 [1841].

Marion, Larry. "The Securities Clearing Time Bomb." *Institutional Investor* (Aug. 1987): 239.

Masera, Rainer S. "Issues in Financial Regulation: Efficiency, Stability, Information." Paper presented at the Société Universitaire Européene de Recherches Financières Colloquium on *Financial Institutions in Europe,* Nice, October 12–14, 1989.

Mayer, Martin. *The Money Bazaars: Understanding the Banking Revolution around Us.* New York: New American Library, 1985.

————. "The Settlements Revolution." *Institutional Investor* (April 1982).

Montagnon, Peter. "How SEK Funds at One Point below LIBOR." *Financial Times,* Dec. 9, 1985, 27.

Multinational Strategies. *Regional Banks: International Strategies for the Future.* New York: MNS, 1987.

Organization for Economic Cooperation and Development. *Financial Market Trends* (March 1985, November 1986, November 1987, May 1989).

Parente, Gioia M. *Critical Issues in the Expansion of the Euronote and Eurocommercial Paper Market.* Salomon Brothers, June 1986.

————. *An Introduction to Note Issuance Facilities.* Salomon Brothers Bond Market Research, 1985.

Prospects for Financial Markets in 1988. Salomon Brothers, December 1987.

"A Risky Business." *Economist,* May 28, 1988, 82.

Shaffer, Sherrill, and David Edmond. "Economies of Superscale and Interstate Expansion." *Federal Reserve Bank of New York,* No. 8612 (Nov. 1986): 1.

Shirreff, David. "Caps and Options." *Euromoney* (March 1986): 26–40.

Soros, George. *Reading the Mind of the Market.* New York: Simon & Schuster, 1988.

S&P's High Yield Quarterly 2(1) (March 15, 1990): 15, 72.

Strange, Susan. *Casino Capitalism.* Oxford: Basil Blackwell, 1986.

Streeter, William W. "What Banking's Coming To." *ABA Banking Journal* (March 1987): 30.

"Survey: International Banking." *Economist*, March 26, 1988, 16.

Walmsley, Julian. *The New Financial Products.* New York: Wiley, 1988.

Wayne, Leslie. "How the Morgan Bank Struck Out." *New York Times,* Feb. 7, 1988, sec. 3, 1.

Index